# First World War
## and Army of Occupation
# War Diary
## France, Belgium and Germany

41 DIVISION
Headquarters, Branches and Services
Commander Royal Engineers
4 May 1916 - 31 October 1917

WO95/2624/1

The Naval & Military Press Ltd
www.nmarchive.com
**Published in association with The National Archives**

Published by

The Naval & Military Press Ltd

Unit 10 Ridgewood Industrial Park,

Uckfield, East Sussex,

TN22 5QE England

Tel: +44 (0) 1825 749494

www.naval-military-press.com

www.nmarchive.com

*This diary has been reprinted in facsimile from the original. Any imperfections are inevitably reproduced and the quality may fall short of modern type and cartographic standards.*

**© Crown Copyright**
**Images reproduced by permission of The National Archives, London, England, 2015.**

# Contents

| Document type | Place/Title | Date From | Date To |
|---|---|---|---|
| Heading | WO95/2624/1 | | |
| Heading | C.R.E. May 1916-1917 Oct 1918 Mar-1919 Oct | | |
| War Diary | Aldershot | 04/05/1916 | 04/05/1916 |
| War Diary | Southampton | 04/05/1916 | 04/05/1916 |
| War Diary | Havre | 05/05/1916 | 06/05/1916 |
| War Diary | Steenbecque | 07/05/1916 | 07/05/1916 |
| War Diary | Merris | 07/05/1916 | 09/05/1916 |
| War Diary | Steenwerck | 10/05/1916 | 30/05/1916 |
| Heading | War Diary For June 1916 Herewith. 8 7/16. | | |
| War Diary | Steenwerck | 01/06/1916 | 12/06/1916 |
| Heading | 41st Div (A) War Diary For July For Base Records. Herewith. | | |
| War Diary | Steenwerck | 01/07/1916 | 28/07/1916 |
| Heading | War Diary. H.Q. R.E. 41st Divn. Month Of August 1916 Vol 4 | | |
| War Diary | Steenwerck | 05/08/1916 | 17/08/1916 |
| War Diary | Fletre | 17/08/1916 | 24/08/1916 |
| War Diary | Ailly | 28/08/1916 | 28/08/1916 |
| War Diary | Dernancourt | 03/09/1916 | 10/09/1916 |
| War Diary | Bellevue Farm Near Albert | 11/09/1916 | 11/09/1916 |
| War Diary | Bellevue Farm | 12/09/1916 | 17/09/1916 |
| War Diary | Ribemont | 18/09/1916 | 28/09/1916 |
| Miscellaneous | Report On The R.E. Operations On 15th, 16th, And 17th September, 1916. | 20/09/1916 | 20/09/1916 |
| War Diary | Ribemont | 01/10/1916 | 01/10/1916 |
| War Diary | Fricourt Chateau | 03/10/1916 | 10/10/1916 |
| War Diary | Buire | 11/10/1916 | 13/10/1916 |
| War Diary | Hillencourt | 16/10/1916 | 18/10/1916 |
| War Diary | Fletre | 19/10/1916 | 19/10/1916 |
| War Diary | Reninghelst | 21/10/1916 | 28/10/1916 |
| Miscellaneous | Report On The R.E. Operations 3rd To 10th October, 1916. | 14/10/1916 | 14/10/1916 |
| Miscellaneous | Operations On The Somme. Total Wastage Of Personnel | 01/11/1916 | 01/11/1916 |
| Miscellaneous | 1st Divisional Engineers Casualties Incurred During Operations On The Somme. | | |
| Operation(al) Order(s) | Operation Order No. 49/2, By Lieut. Col. E.N. Stockley. C.R.E. 41st. Division. | 08/10/1916 | 08/10/1916 |
| War Diary | Reninghelst | 02/11/1916 | 28/11/1916 |
| Miscellaneous | Orders By C.R.E. 41st. Division. 19-11-1915. | 19/11/1916 | 19/11/1916 |
| War Diary | Reninghelst | 11/12/1916 | 27/12/1916 |
| War Diary | | 14/12/1916 | 14/12/1916 |
| Miscellaneous | A Form. Messages And Signals. | | |
| War Diary | Reninghelst | 01/01/1917 | 22/06/1917 |
| War Diary | Westoutre | 23/06/1917 | 30/06/1917 |
| Miscellaneous | Report on the R.E. and Pioneer Operations on 7th, 8th, and 9th June, 1917. | 09/06/1917 | 09/06/1917 |
| Miscellaneous | 141st Infantry Brigade. Intelligence Report Canal & Spoil Bank Sub-Sectors Appendix 11 | | |

| Type | Description | Start | End |
|---|---|---|---|
| Miscellaneous | 141st Infantry Brigade. Intelligence Report Canal & Spoil Bank Sub-Sectors | 02/06/1917 | 02/06/1917 |
| Miscellaneous | 141st Infantry Brigade. Intelligence Report Canal & Spoil Bank Sub-Sector | | |
| Miscellaneous | 141st Infantry Brigade. Intelligence Report Canal Sub-Sectors | | |
| Operation(al) Order(s) | 141st Infantry Brigade. Intelligence Report | | |
| Miscellaneous | 141st Infantry Brigade. Intelligence Report | 11/06/1917 | 11/06/1917 |
| Miscellaneous | 141st Infantry Brigade. Intelligence Report | 12/06/1917 | 12/06/1917 |
| Map | | | |
| Miscellaneous | Message | | |
| Miscellaneous | | 04/08/1917 | 04/08/1917 |
| Miscellaneous | | | |
| Miscellaneous | Report On The R.E. And Pioneer Operations On 31st July, 1st & 2nd August, 1917. | | |
| War Diary | Near Berthen Sheet. 27. R 21.a.2.8. | 01/07/1917 | 18/07/1917 |
| War Diary | Near Berthen | 18/07/1917 | 24/07/1917 |
| War Diary | Westoutre | 25/07/1917 | 31/07/1917 |
| Miscellaneous | O.C. 228th Field Coy. R.E. O.C. 233rd Field Coy. R.E. O.C. 237th Field Coy. R.E. 41st Div. "G". 41st Div. "Q". C.R.A. 41st Divn. 122nd Infantry Brigade. 123rd Infantry Brigade. 124th Infantry Brigade. | 23/07/1917 | 23/07/1917 |
| Miscellaneous | 123rd Infantry Brigade. O.C. 233rd Field Coy. R.E. (For information). | 20/07/1917 | 20/07/1917 |
| Operation(al) Order(s) | 41st Divisional Engineers Operation Order No. H.Z.2. | 29/07/1917 | 29/07/1917 |
| War Diary | Westoutre | 01/08/1917 | 15/08/1917 |
| War Diary | Berthen | 16/08/1917 | 21/08/1917 |
| War Diary | Wizernes | 24/08/1917 | 31/08/1917 |
| Miscellaneous | 41st Divisional Engineers. | | |
| Map | Plan-Illustrating-Work-As-Per Detailed-Report. | | |
| War Diary | Wizernes | 03/09/1917 | 03/09/1917 |
| War Diary | La Clyte | 05/09/1917 | 14/09/1917 |
| War Diary | Zevecoten | 15/09/1917 | 21/09/1917 |
| War Diary | Caestre | 23/09/1917 | 26/09/1917 |
| War Diary | La Panne | 28/09/1917 | 28/09/1917 |
| Miscellaneous | 41st Divisional Engineers. | 01/05/1916 | 01/05/1916 |
| Miscellaneous | Casualties. Attched Infantry. | | |
| Operation(al) Order(s) | C.R.E's Operation Order No. T.H.2. | 18/09/1917 | 18/09/1917 |
| War Diary | La Panne | 01/10/1917 | 07/10/1917 |
| War Diary | St Idesbald | 08/10/1917 | 29/10/1917 |
| War Diary | Malo Les Bains | 30/10/1917 | 31/10/1917 |
| Operation(al) Order(s) | C.R.E's Operation Order C.S. No. 1. | 04/10/1917 | 04/10/1917 |
| Operation(al) Order(s) | C.R.E's Operation Order C.S. No. 2. | 09/10/1917 | 09/10/1917 |
| Miscellaneous | Programme Of Work In Forward Area East Of Cost Dunkerke-Cost Dunkerke Bains Road. | | |
| Miscellaneous | Programme Of Hutting Work West Of The Coxyde-Coxyde Bains Road. | | |
| Miscellaneous | Programme Of Hutting And Defence Work East Of Coxyde-Coxyde Bains Road. | | |
| Operation(al) Order(s) | C.R.E's Operation Order C.S. No. 3. | 11/10/1917 | 11/10/1917 |
| Operation(al) Order(s) | C.R.E's Operation Order C.S. No. 4. | 11/10/1917 | 11/10/1917 |
| Miscellaneous | Distribution Of Divisional Engineers For Operations. Appendix I. | | |
| Map | | | |

W09/
2624(1)

# 41ST DIVISION

## C. R. E.

MAY 1916-~~DEC 1918~~ 1917 OCT

1918 MAR - 1919 OCT

1917 NOV to 1918 FEB } ITALY

DUPLICATE
Army Form C. 2118

41st Div. R.E. H'quarters

# WAR DIARY
or
## INTELLIGENCE SUMMARY
(Erase heading not required.)

Instructions regarding War Diaries and Intelligence Summaries are contained in F.S. Regs., Part II. and the Staff Manual respectively. Title Pages will be prepared in manuscript.

| Place | Date | Hour | Summary of Events and Information | Remarks and references to Appendices |
|---|---|---|---|---|
| ALDERSHOT | May 4th | 3.45 p.m. | Headquarters Div'l R.E. entrained at FARNBOROUGH, S.W.R. The C.R.E., 1st Lt W.M. Coldstream R.E. and one driver, his batman did not entrain owing to sudden serious illness of C.R.E. | |
| SOUTHAMPTON | " | 5 p.m. | Detrained and embarked on steamer "Huanchaco" under difficulties owing to lack of personnel. | |
| | " | 8.15 p.m. | Sailed, and arrived at HAVRE 9.00 a.m. May 5th | |
| HAVRE | May 5th | 9.30 a.m. 2.15 p.m. | Disembarked and moved to No 1 Rest Camp | |
| " | 6th | 12 noon 2.45 p.m. | Entrained at Gare des Marchandises, Point No 1 | |
| STEEN-BECQUE | 7th | 10.30 a.m. | Detrained and marched to MERRIS arriving at 5.30 p.m. | |
| MERRIS | 7th | 8 p.m. | Capt. G.E. Baker R.E. commanding 228th Fd. C.o.R.E. under instructions from H.Q. 2nd 41st Division took over the duties of C.R.E. | |
| " | 8th | | Acting C.R.E. and Adjt. went to STEENWERCK to confer with C.R.E. 9th Div." regarding taking over the line held by 9th Div". Attended staff conference at 41st Div'l Head Brs in the evening | |

# WAR DIARY
## or
## INTELLIGENCE SUMMARY
*(Erase heading not required.)*

Army Form C. 2118

Instructions regarding War Diaries and Intelligence Summaries are contained in F. S. Regs., Part II. and the Staff Manual respectively. Title Pages will be prepared in manuscript.

| Place | Date | Hour | Summary of Events and Information | Remarks and references to Appendices |
|---|---|---|---|---|
| MERRIS | May 9th | | Again went to Steenwerk and went around shops and field company billets of R.E. 9th Divn. with C.R.E. 9th Divn. | |
| STEENWERK | 10th | | Attended conference at 41st Divn. Hd Qrs. in evening | |
| | 11th | | Hd Qrs. Divl. R.E. moved from MERRIS to STEEN WERK. Conferred with C.R.E. 9th Divn. | |
| | 12th | | at C.R.E. and adjt. went around army and corps workshops and R.E. Park at Hazebrouck, Ballieul and Strazeele. | |
| | 13th | | Went around trenches of right sector and part of centre sector trenches held by 9th Divn. with C.R.E. 9th Divn. | |
| | | | Went around grenade and trench training school with C.R.E. 9th Divn. and around left sector trenches with a representative of the field company in charge of that part of the line. | |
| | 14th | | Went around the field company billets and conferred with the O.C. of the field company now employing the left sector. Visited Hd Qrs 41st Divn. at MERRIS. Lt. Col. E. N. Stockley has been appointed C.R.E. of this Divn. | |

# WAR DIARY or INTELLIGENCE SUMMARY

Army Form C. 2118

| Place | Date | Hour | Summary of Events and Information | Remarks and references to Appendices |
|---|---|---|---|---|
| STEENWERK | Mar 15 | | Lieut Colonel E.N. STOCKLEY R.E. (visited for duty as CRE 41st Divn) | |
| | 16 | | Visiting all sectors of the line with CRE 9th Divn | |
| | " | | CRE 41st Divn took over charge of work on the line from CRE 9th Divn at midday 11-22/23 | |
| | 22 | | | |
| | 20 | | Lieut Col Roberts 19th Middlesex Regt (Pioneers) took charge of that RE Park. Armentières | |
| | 20 | | Lieut HE Billang | Divl C Hutting Yard. NIEPPE. |
| | 23 | | Capt H.S. Emery | French tramways |
| | 29 | | Lieut HV Slayter | Drainage |
| | 30 | | G.O.C. 41st Divn. took over command of the line from G.O.C. 9th Divn 11.9 pm | |
| | | | Order of Battle. Left Sector *122nd Infy Bde with 228th Field Co. R.E. affiliated | |
| | | | Centre Sector *124th Infy Bde with 237 — " — | |
| | | | Right Sector *123rd Infy Bde with 233 — " — | |
| | | | * Brigades lying in turn ① 2 Bns in front line 2 in reserve alternating | |
| | | | R.E. Field Companies Tramways frequently in their sectors viz — | |
| | | | 228 Coy F.T. 127 to 121 (PERRES POINT to BIRDCAGE) | |
| | | | 237 " " 120 to 103 (BIRDCAGE to WARNAVE) | |
| | | | 233 " " 102 to 90 (WARNAVE to R. LYS) | |

SN Stockley Lieut Col
CRE 41st Divn

War diary
for June 1916
herewith.

8/7/16. R R G Perkins
for C.E.

Adjt: C.R.E. 41st Divn:

**Army Form C. 2118**

# WAR DIARY
## or
## INTELLIGENCE SUMMARY
*(Erase heading not required.)*

Instructions regarding War Diaries and Intelligence Summaries are contained in F. S. Regs., Part II. and the Staff Manual respectively: Title Pages will be prepared in manuscript.

June 1916 — H.Q. 41st Div.E. Regn 2218

Vol 2 Jeune

| Place | Date | Hour | Summary of Events and Information | Remarks and references to Appendices |
|---|---|---|---|---|
| STEENWERCK | JUNE 1st | | Chief Engineer 2nd Corps visited works in Left Sector. | |
| | 5th | | Right Sector. | |
| | 10th | | Centre Sector. | |
| | 19th | | 2nd Corps H.Q.s left this area and handed over to V. Corps | |
| | 30th | | V. Corps handed over Corps as well as divisional work to H.Q. 2nd Corps area. | |
| | 14th | | CRE Lieut Col ENTWISTLE proceeded on short leave to England H.Q. 21st Divis carried on by Capt E.C. Baker | |
| | 5th | | Capt W.E. Day was killed in T.96 by a sniper bullet wound in head. | |
| | 18th | | Capt H.F.O. Thwaites from 42nd A.T. Coy.R.E. appointed to command 233rd Field Coy, vice Capt Day | |
| | 6th | | Lieut R.J. Wicker (wounded) was evacuated to the Base for England. | |
| | 12th | | 2nd Lieut R.H. Chapman joined 237th Field Coy. vice Lieut Wicker. | |

During the month the 3 Field Companies R.E. continued at work in the lines. The principal works carried out being the remodelling, resisting and constructing new main communication trenches — Reclaiming and resisting the S.P. & C.P. line — Constructing additional support in Ksent line breastworks — Constructing M.G. Immediate Aug.mts and S.P. and Concrete M.G. Emp. for advanced Front trenches and Brigade Hdqrs — New advanced dressing stations. Sapping in front of the line at trenches 125, 126, 127 to advance to line. Wiring to shield previous of work 3 sections attached from Pioneer to work in the Right and Centre Sectors.

S.M. Moseley Lieut Col R.E.
C.R.E. 41st Divis.

8-7-16.

CONFIDENTIAL.

41st Divn (A.)

War Diary for
July for Base Records,
herewith.

28/16

Adjt: /C.R.E. 41st Divn:

Army Form C. 2118

# WAR DIARY
or
# INTELLIGENCE SUMMARY
(Erase heading not required.)

Hdqrs. 41st Divn: Engineers —
July 1916              Vol 3

| Place | Date | Hour | Summary of Events and Information | Remarks and references to Appendices |
|---|---|---|---|---|
| STEENWERCK | 1st | | The 41st Divn: front being extensive to the north to the R. Douve the 235th Field Company was moved from ARMENTIÈRES to LE ROMARIN has to take over the work in the new Left Sector — The work of the three field Companies was thus redistributed as under— Left Sector   R. Douve to Trench 128, with 3 main C.T.s ASH LANE, THE ONLY AVE, ANNISTRAST AVENUE. Centre Sector  Trench 127 to Trench 121 with 3 main C.T.S. ONTARIO AVENUE – TORONTO AVENUE – THE STRAND. Right Sector  Trench 120 to Trench 112 with 4 main C.T.s PICCADILLY, HAYMARKET, LOWNDES AVENUE, BORDER AVENUE Capt Fielding was attached as R.E. liaison officer to the 123rd Brigade holding Trench 113 & the R.L.Y.S as his arranging the Left R.E. Company to work on that front — | |
| | 3rd | | Lieut F.T. Tomlinson Field Engineer was temporarily attached to 47th Divn as Assist. works Army Commander in the Corps area pending his transfer to S. Downs by the 42nd A.T. Coy R.E. 145th A.T. Coy R.E. the 49th A.T. Coy R.E. and civil labour. | |
| | 16th | | The advanced billet of the section of 237 Field Coy at Mont's Farm was shelled & vacated & 2nd Lieut T.R. Stratton and Sergt R.T. Hodder were recommended for Gallantry or Distinction N.97106 Sergt Hodder A.T. awarded Military Medal. | |
| | 14th | | Lieut Carlin 228 F Coy slightly wounded, remained at duty — | |
| | 14th | | Lieut S.R. Toms 237 F Coy appointed Brigade Engineer II Corps replaced by ...... who joined for duty 19.7.16 | |
| | 25th | | Lieut A.F. Kistler 228 F Coy wounded and evacuated to England replaced by ...... who joined for duty 28.7.16 | |

# Army Form C. 2118

## WAR DIARY
## or
## INTELLIGENCE SUMMARY
(Erase heading not required.)

Instructions regarding War Diaries and Intelligence Summaries are contained in F. S. Regs., Part II. and the Staff Manual respectively. Title Pages will be prepared in manuscript.

| Place | Date | Hour | Summary of Events and Information | Remarks and references to Appendices |
|---|---|---|---|---|
| | 26. | | Apart 2 NCOs & Sappers of the 237 F. Coy took part in a raid against the enemys Trenches. Cpl Cuthbert. G. was recommended for great gallantry on this occasion, for out of the Eight Sappers who were wounded but this charges were placed in time and he stair and assisted his successfully completed. Cpl Cuthbert himself also was wounded twice his party in and then returned to help in his & his comrades rescue. — The Division al front having been ordered to extend from Issues 127 to the R.Lys) the 233rd Field Coy was moved back to British ARMENTIÈRES formed & TSH Sector and the Field Coys were reallotted to Sectors with their offices as Brigades viz. | |
| | | | Right Sector 233rd F. Coy with 123rd Bde. Issues 102 to R.Lys |  |
| | | | Centre Sector 237. F. Coy with 124. Bde. Issues 103 to 120 |  |
| | | | Left Sector 225. F. Coy with 122 Bde. Issues 121 to 127 |  |
| | 28. | | During the month the C.Rs continued on main Communication Trenches. Relaying & strutting to S, & S2 Lines. Advanced Report Centres. Staff and R.A.H5. O.Ps. Advanced Dressing Stations and Regtl Aid Posts. Stokes Gun Emplacements. A F.S.L. Companion Book was issued 28.7.16 which included the complete relocation marking and rais in the front line for works in occupation with Supervision Tracer — all Communication trenches also to Complete the S, & S2 Line with drys not a communication line Battalion. Emplacements? on steel & concrete shell-proof dug outs re-stocking with W.C. | 2-8-16 CRE 41st Divn |

Original — — Confidential —

Vol 4

# War Diary.

## H.Q. R.E. 41st Divn.

— Month of August —
— 1916 —

# WAR DIARY
## or
## INTELLIGENCE SUMMARY

Army Form C. 2118

HdQrs 41st Divl Engrs

August 1916

| Place | Date | Hour | Summary of Events and Information | Remarks and references to Appendices |
|---|---|---|---|---|
| STEENWERCK | 5 | | The Saps from Trenches 125, 126, 127 were joined up by fire trench during the night of 5/6th and the fire trench deepened with firestep the night of 6/7th mining in front of the new trenches was completed. The work was very carefully organized by Capt Baker 228th Ey. with Lieut Berry and 2nd Lieut Stratton each in charge of working parties in his subsections. Very few casualties occurred and the trenches and CTs are being formed and breastwork parapet raised to form a permanent trench suitable for winter occupation if required. | |
| | 6 | | The NIEPPE Hutting yard was heavily shelled & had 6 evacuates. | |
| | 7 | | New RE Divisional Park and Workshops laid out at TROIS ARBRES (just north of the BAILLEUL ARMENTIERES Railway line at B.13.G.Central (map 36) - Railway siding with bogard(?) on ccrd(?) and Tram lines to connect to RE Company billets at DOUDOU Cr & LEURIDON and the Trench tramway system in PLOEGSTREET wood - | |
| | 8 | | CRE visited the positions on the SOMME on XV Corps front 33rd Divl area. | |

# WAR DIARY
## or
## INTELLIGENCE SUMMARY

August 1916 (2)

| Place | Date | Hour | Summary of Events and Information | Remarks and references to Appendices |
|---|---|---|---|---|
| STEENWERCK | 14th to 17th | | CRE & Adj'r 23rd Divn paid daily visits with Shewn round all works in progress. Workshops Stores preparatory to handing over. | |
| FLETRE | 17th | | HeadQrs H.1st Divn Moved to visit billets at FLETRE. | |
| | 18th to 22nd | | The Field Companies were located at billets as under: | |
| | | | 228th F. Coy at MOOLNACKER Map 27 x 19 a.3.8 | |
| | | | 233rd " Coy — 27 x 26. 6. 0 | |
| | | | 237th F. Coy at LES ORMES — 27 x 14 c.7.3 | |
| | | | Daily route marching and drill when Cannes out. Also practice with the Sentinel Hydraulic pipe forcing jack — Each Company arranged athletic sports with H.Q.r Company events — | |
| | 23rd | | H.Q 2 Entrained at BRILLEUL for LONGPRE en route for AILLY (LE HAUT CLOCHER) | |
| | 24th | | H.Qrs detrained at LONGPRE and marched to AILLY (LE HAUT CLOCHER) | |
| | | | The Field Coys were located at 228th F. Coy BOUCHON | |
| | | | 233rd " F. Coy ERGNIES | |
| | | | 237 F. Coy FAUCOURT SUR SOMME | |
| | | | Training was carried out in consolidation of trench, forming wiring strong points and overturning. | |

# WAR DIARY or INTELLIGENCE SUMMARY

Army Form C. 2118

Title Pages August 1916 (3)

| Place | Date | Hour | Summary of Events and Information | Remarks and references to Appendices |
|---|---|---|---|---|
| AILLY | 28th | | H.Qrs. and 2 Sections 237th F.Coy. moved to FLEXICOURT to join the IVth Army School of instruction in trench warfare. | |
| | 1.9.16 | | | |

J.M.Rocker Lieut Col R.E.
CRE 41st Divn

Army Form C. 2118

# WAR DIARY
## or
## INTELLIGENCE SUMMARY

H.Q.s 41st Div. Engineers

Sept 1916

(Erase heading not required.)

Instructions regarding War Diaries and Intelligence Summaries are contained in F.S. Regs, Part II. and the Staff Manual respectively. Title Pages will be prepared in manuscript.

| Place | Date | Hour | Summary of Events and Information | Remarks and references to Appendices |
|---|---|---|---|---|
| DERNANCOURT | 3rd | | H.Q.s R.E. moved from AILLY to DERNAN COURT and the Field Companies moved up by train and march route to FRICOURT – | |
| | 5th | | The 41st Div. R.E and PIONEERS were placed under the orders of the XV Corps for preliminary work for the resumption of the offensive in front of FLERS – Work was commenced on two main communication trenches leading forward from MONTAUBAN ALLEY to the front line on either side of LONGUEVAL. MILK LANE to junction with PONT STREET in S11c. = 2050 yards. PIPPE LANE to junction with DEVIL'S TRENCH in S11d. = 3100 yards These trenches are to be dug to a width 7'½ cover 3' and to provide 7'½ cover. The floor of the trenches together – Runners posts each for 1 NCO & 6 men to be provided every 500 x two hundred. Bde H.Q.s were also to be provided in YORK TRENCH. The work to be all complete by provide by the 70th division – | |
| | 6.9.16 | | Work was continued with day and night parties and good progress made – | |
| BELLEVUE FARM near ALBERT. | 11th | | The 41st Div. took over the Centre Sector of the XV Corps front at 8 am. H.Qrs R.E moved up to join Div. H.Qrs" – the R.E Pioneers came under the orders of the Division to continue the preparatory work on which they were employed. Carrying to Main C.Ts forward to the front line and making up existing trenches and alternative routes – | |

# WAR DIARY or INTELLIGENCE SUMMARY

Army Form C. 2118

Sept. 1916    2nd Sheet

| Place | Date | Hour | Summary of Events and Information | Remarks and references to Appendices |
|---|---|---|---|---|
| BELLEVUE FARM | 12th | | On the night of the 11/12th the front line of the Division was advanced 100' to 750' to within 200' of the SUPPORT TRENCH breastwork of the enemy on the front line. This work was carried out by Capt THWAITES with 2 sections of K.O.S.B. 255th Bty and a working party of 3 Coys of 2 Infantry with 1 Coy as covering party. 5 Strong Points were constructed on the left of the LONGUEVAL PIERS road and 4 Strong Points on the right of the road. LIEUT. N.D.R. HUNTER who was in charge of the work to the left of the road was slightly wounded and displayed gallantry in bringing in his section. Sappers who had been severely wounded when returning to the front to resume charge of the work after he had hastily had his own wounds — LIEUT. CRAVER was in charge of the work on the right of the road. The R.E. sections were issued stretchers as drawn learning to carry forward to make front and connect to chain 2 Strong Points. | |
| | 13th | | Work in C.T.S. BETWEEN RESERVE TRENCH was continued. The R.E. Officers were held responsible from work were assembled in his opinion in advance of the line at MONTAUBAN. One section from each Coy was attached to the Infantry brigades. | |
| | 14th | | | |
| | 15th | | The 41st Div attacked and captured the village of FLERS. A special report on the operation of the 15th 16th 17th is attached. | |

# WAR DIARY or INTELLIGENCE SUMMARY

Army Form C. 2118

Third Sheet —

Sept. 1916

| Place | Date | Hour | Summary of Events and Information | Remarks and references to Appendices |
|---|---|---|---|---|
| BELLEVUE FARM | 16th | | On the night of the 15th/16th Capt. BAKER proceeded with 3 Section 228th Coy, 2 Sections 237 Coy and 1 Section 253rd Coy to consolidate the position in front of FLERS — Capt. F.C. BAKER and Lieut. T.B. BATTY were severely wounded before reaching the position and Capt. C.L.T. MATESON took command of the party. Consolidating the front line on the right of FLERS VILLAGE and forming strong points on the flanks with a machine gun position on the extreme right flank. Two Section works at the same two. Two sections were employed in consolidating a portion of the FLERS TRENCH between FLERS and FOURCELINE. Two sections employed in consolidating the SWITCH TRENCH — as a front line — | |
| | | | The two remaining sections were employed on the 16th in improving the MONTAUBAN — RUPPERY road which was used for bringing up supplies from the R.O.'s at RUPPERY. | |
| | 17th | | On the night of the 16th/17th four sections under command of Capt. THWAITE'S proceeded to the front of FLERS and consolidated the w's 2 Sentry Strong Points — BOX — COX — HOG'S HEAD covering the front of the village. Two sections continued the work on FLERS TRENCH and the section in SWITCH TRENCH. The remaining sections were employed on the 17th on the MONTAUBAN — RUPPERY road. The PIONEERS on the 15th, 16th, 17th were employed on clearing and improving the forward roads for light traffic i.e. in the GREEN DUMP — WINDMILL — DUKE ST. LONGUEVAL road and 3 Coys on the MONTAUBAN — BRONN DUMP — LONGUEVAL road — On the afternoon of the 17th the Field Companies and Pioneers were withdrawn to Camp at RICOURT. | |

**Army Form C. 2118**

# WAR DIARY
## or
## INTELLIGENCE SUMMARY

(Erase heading not required.)

Sept 1916  Fourth Sheet

Instructions regarding War Diaries and Intelligence Summaries are contained in F. S. Regs., Part II. and the Staff Manual respectively. Title Pages will be prepared in manuscript.

| Place | Date | Hour | Summary of Events and Information | Remarks and references to Appendices |
|---|---|---|---|---|
| RIBEMONT | 18th | | The 41st Div. was relieved at 9PM and H.Q.s moved back from BELLEVUE FARM to RIBEMONT. 6th Coys remained in Camp at FRICOURT for rest. | |
| | 20th | | The Divisional Commander ordered a parade of the 3 Field Coys and complied section 72nd in their good work during the operations of the 15th-17th and the preliminary work done prior to the attack which has said had materially assisted in the success gained by the 41st Div. | |
| | 21st | | The Field Coys were again placed under the orders of C.E. xv Corps. | |
| | 22nd | | Field Co. Camps moved from FRICOURT to MONTAUBAN and H.Q. Commenced a move to secure access to the ROAD Supply Materials at MONTAUBAN. | |
| | 23rd | | Lieut. E. Stouton Kaisdale was slightly wounded in BERNAFAY WOOD whilst setting limits for the road. | |
| | 28th | | 233rd Field Coy R.E. detailed for temporary duty with 2nd Dn. on construction of main CT east of FLERS village up to GIRD TRENCH. | |
| | 1.10.16 | | | |

J McCulley Lieut GnRL
CRE 41st Div

SECRET

41 Div.
G.430.

REPORT ON THE R.E. OPERATIONS ON 15TH, 16TH,
AND 17TH SEPTEMBER, 1916.

On the night of the 14/15th the R.E. were disposed as under:-

In bivouacs near MONTAUBAN.
Hd.Qrs. and 3 Sections 228th Field Coy.  Capt. E.C.Baker
Hd.Qrs. and 3 Sections 233rd Field Coy.  Capt. H.F.O.Thwaites
Hd.Qrs. and 3 Sections 237th Field Coy.  Capt. C.L.T. Matheson

The Field Companies having left camp at FRICOURT F.9.c. Central at 7.15.p.m. with only section transport. One section 228th Field Coy. R.E. under Lieut. E.T.G.Carter was detached under orders of the G.O.C. 122nd Infantry Brigade, and reported to him at YORK TRENCH at 7.0.p.m. This section then taped out assembly lines for the Brigade, the Division behind and parellel to our front line in 3 lines about 480 yards lay at 70 yards spacing. The section then retrned to near Brigade H.Q. at GREEN DUMP.
No further orders were received till 8.0.a.m. on the 15th, when orders were given to get into touch with the O.C. Front line of troops and assist in consolidating Strong Points round FLERS. The section then proceeded to S.6.b.1.8. and constructed a Strong Point, without Infantry assistance.
At about 2.0p.m. the Brigade Major ordered Lieut. Carter to assemble all the scattered parties of Infantry and take them with his sappers round the right of FLERS VILLAGE, saying that he himself was taking a party round the left and would meet him on the other side. Lieut. Carter again met the Brigade Major at about W.31. central and received further instructions to occupy "COX". This he did and proceeded to consolidate the position without infantry assistance. No covering party was provided. At about 5.0.p.m. word was passed down from the right to stand to. Lieut. Carter went along to the right to find the source of this order and found the supporting infantry had retired and were going away out of sight up the valley. Being thus left in the air, Lieut. Carter decided to withdraw his section and moved back and reported to the Brigade at YORK TRENCH. His section of 32 men having suffered 14 casualties. After remaining the night at GREEN DUMP, he received orders at 7.0.a.m. to return to the Company bivouac.

One section 237th Field Company was detached under the orders of the G.O.C. 124 Brigade and reported at YORK TRENCH at 8.0.p.m.
It was subdivided by Brigade orders into 2 half sections, one half section under Lieut. Hunter was ordered to report to the O.C. 26th Royal Fusiliers, and the other half under Sergt. Mossman was ordered to report to the O.C. 32nd Royal Fusiliers, both in EDGE TRENCH.
The section then proceeded to EDGE TRENCH, and finding no one there, went on to GREEN TRENCH, where they waited till 5.0.a.m. until the infantry arrived. The first battalion to arrive was the 26th Royal Fusiliers, and Lieut. Hunter accompanied them with 14 men

Sergt. Mosaman was left in GREEN TRENCH with the remaining 14 men, and accompanied a party of the 15th Hants, who appeared in GREEN TRENCH, in accordance with the order of the officer with the party, as far as SWITCH TRENCH, where he reported to the O.C. 15th Hants, who ordered him to put in two machine gun emplacements and a fire step in the trench. This was done with infantry assistance. On reporting completion of the work to Col. Cary Barnard, he was ordered to return and report to his Company. This he did at 1.30.p.m. on the 15th. Lieut. Hunter in the meantime reported to Col. North the O.C. 26th Royal Fusiliers, and assisted the Infantry in consolidating in SWITCH TRENCH. On completion, the O.C. 26th Royal Fusiliers ordered him to return, and he reported to the Brigade Headquarter in YORK TRENCH, who said they had no further orders. He accordingly reported to the O.C. 237th Field Co. R.E. at 4.0.p.m. on the 15th.

One section of the 233rd Field Coy. R.E. was ordered to report at POMMIERS REDOUBT at 8.0.p.m. to the G.O.C. 123rd Infantry Brigade, and Lieut. Langdale, who was in command, received instructions to report to the O.C. 10th R.W.Kents. The section bivouaced with the R.W.Kents till 12.30.a.m. on the 15th, when the party moved from YORK TRENCH, arriving there at 3.30.a.m.
No further instructions were received till 12.15.p.m. when the battalion moved to the junction of MILK LANE and CARLTON TRENCH, when they waited till 2.30.p.m. when the section received orders to advance between "B" and "C" Companies and consolidate in SWITCH TRENCH. The section advanced among the various parties of the R.W.Kents, and reached TEA TRENCH at about S.11.a.4.4. Lieut. Langdale then reported to O.C. Battalion, who appeared to be under the impression he had reached SWITCH TRENCH. Lieut. Langdale then carried out a reconnaissance with a section sergeant as far as SWITCH TRENCH, and sent back the sergeant as a guide for the O.C. Battalion, who brought up a part of his battalion and the sappers to SWITCH TRENCH. At about S.5.a.7.2. Col. Woodmartin, who had given intructions to a part of his battalion to move to the right about 800 yards and was then about to recall parties who had straggled further off towards HIGH WOOD was wounded; by the time Lieut. Langdale and one private had bound him up, all the infantry had disappeared. Lieut. Langdale then went to the forward dressing station at S.11.c.0.5. and sent up a stretcher for him. Lieut. Langdale then turned up towards SWITCH TRENCH and rendez-voused his sappers at the junction of MILK LANE and CARLTON TRENCH reporting to Capt. Thwaites on his arrival at about 7.0.p.m. on the 15th, who then took charge of the halfsection with the other two sections that he was taking up for consolidating work in rear of FLERS. In the meantime Corpl. Rice with half a section had moved with the right column of the 10th R.W.Kents, and assisted the infantry in consolidation of a portion of SWITCH TRENCH on the West of the LONGUEVAL - FLERS Road.
At about 9.0.p.m. the work in hand was completed and no officer being present, Corpl. Rice returned with his sappers to Company Headquarters and reported himself.

The remainder of the R.E. acted under Divisional orders conveyed through the C.R.E. on the night of 15/16th.
Capt. Baker was ordered to proceed with the remaining 3 sections of his Company, 2 sections of the 237th Field Company and

one section of the 233rd Company to consolidate the line
BOX - COX - HOGSHEAD in front of FLERS.
In front of LONGUEVAL, Capt. Baker and Lieut. Berry were
severely wounded and Capt. Matheson took command of the
six sections.
Information being received that no line in front of FLERS
was held, Capt. Matheson then reconnoitred to ascertain
where the front line was. Finding that the infantry had
fallen back from HOGSHEAD and that the front line was on
the right of FLERS from N.31.c.8.8. to N.31.d.6.6. he
consolidated this line, making Strong Points on each flank,
and one central one with also a machine gun emplacement on
the right return flank. The work being completed at about
1.0.a.m. One section of the 237th Company and one section
of the 233rd Company were left to consolidate in the BROWN LINE
in accordance with instructions. Two sections of the 233rd
Company, under command of Capt. Thwaites were employed at
the same time consolidating behind the line of FLERS TRENCH
behind FLERS. In continuation of the work carried out by
Lieut. Carter in the day time using the old wire of FLERS
TRENCH as an obstacle.

On the 16th the two sections who had not yet been employed
worked on the improvement of the MONTAUBAN - QUARRY Road
which was being used for evacuation of the wounded from the
advanced dressing station.

On the night of the 16/17th four sections under command of
Capt. Thwaites were ordered to proceed to FLERS to report
to the commandant of FLERS.(Major OTTER) and consolidated the
line BOX - COX - HOGSHEAD. Finding BOX occupied by the
troops of the New Zealand Division, work was concentrated in
COX and HOGSHEAD, and on completing the gaps in a connecting
trench, which the infantry had dug, also in making a short
length of C.T. back to the SUNKEN ROAD. The two sections at
work in the BROWN LINE were ordered to be relieved and one
additional section was sent to the GREEN LINE to work till
4.0.a.m. On the 17th these sections were again employed on
the MONTAUBAN - QUARRY Road.

On the afternoon of the 17th all the Companies were withdrawn
to camp at FRICOURT.

The lessons learned as regards R.E.Work are:-

1. That R.E. should as far as possible be employed under the
direct orders of the Division on definite work of tactical
value. The sections given to the brigades were left almost
entirely on their own initiative without any definite instruction

2. No party of R.E. of less size than a section under an
officer should be employed, except perhaps a few guides who
would be very useful to show the infantry the way, and avoid
the confusion which occurred through the lack of knowledge of
the trenches and of the direction of the attack. These should
rejoin their sections at once.

3. A preliminary engineer reconnaissance of the positions
to be consolidated before the night parties of R.E. are sent
out, would be very helpful in deciding what number of men, tools
and materials are likely to be required.

4. One stretcher per R.E.Section should be carried. the Regimental stretcher bearer system is very apt to leave out the R.E. who have no stretcher bearers of their own. If two stretcher bearers per section could be added supernumerary to the strength, they would be very useful in other ways.

5. For tool transport, the pack cobs were found very useful, the conditions were impossibel for getting tool carts forward. This suggested that a second pack saddle per section should be carried for us on a spare horse or cob. This would enable one pick and shovel for each man to be carried so that the sappers could each carry up 25 sandbags for consolidation work.
In only one case was an infantry carrying party provided, and so that the sappers had to rely on what they could bring or find themselves.

6. Generally, the infantry do not appear yet to appreciate the tactical value of the sappers; and except where they were employed directly under Divisional orders with a Company Commander incharge, their work was apt to be misdirected. Probably, therefore, in working with a new army, especially as the junior or temporary R.E. officers are apt themselves to be lacking in Military experience, it is best to work the Field Companies, as far as possible, as complete units.

(Signed) E.N.Stockley,
Lieut. Col. R.E.
20.9.16.   C.R.E. 41st Division.

SECRET

41 Div.
G.430.

REPORT ON THE R.E. OPERATIONS ON 15TH, 16TH,
AND 17TH SEPTEMBER, 1916.
----------------------------------

On the night of the 14/15th the R.E. were disposed as under:-

In bivouacs near MONTAUBAN.
Hd.Qrs. and 3 Sections 228th Field Coy.    Capt. E.C.Baker
Hd.Qrs. and 3 Sections 233rd Field Coy.    Capt. H.F.O.Thwaites
Hd.Qrs. and 3 Sections 237th Field Coy.    Capt. C.L.T. Matheson

The Field Companies having left camp at FRICOURT F.9.c. Central at 7.15.p.m. with only section transport. One section 228th Field Coy. R.E. under Lieut. E.T.G.Carter was detached under orders of the G.O.C. 122nd Infantry Brigade, and reported to him at YORK TRENCH at 7.0.p.m. This section then taped out assembly lines for the Brigade, the Division behind and parellel to our front line in 3 lines about 480 yards lay at 70 yards spacing. The section then retrned to near Brigade H.Q. at GREEN DUMP.
No further orders were received till 8.0.a.m. on the 15th, when orders were given to get into touch with the O.C. Front line of troops and assist in consolidating Strong Points round FLERS. The section then proceeded to S.6.b.1.8. and constructed a Strong Point, without Infantry assistance.
At about 2.0p.m. the Brigade Major ordered Lieut. Carter to assemble all the scattered parties of Infantry and take them with his sappers round the right of FLERS VILLAGE, saying that he himself was taking a party round the left and would meet him on the other side. Lieut. Carter again met the Brigade Major at about W.31. central and received further instructions to occupy "COX". This he did and proceeded to consolidate the position without infantry assistance. No covering party was provided. At about 5.0.p.m. word was passed down from the right to stand to. Lieut. Carter went along to the right to find the source of this order and found the supporting infantry had retired and were going away out of sight up the valley. Being thus left in the air, Lieut. Carter decided to withdraw his section and moved back and reported to the Brigade at YORK TRENCH. His section of 32 men having suffered 14 casualties. After remaining the night at GREEN DUMP, he received orders at 7.0.a.m. to return to the Company bivouac.

One section 237th Field Company was detached under the orders of the G.O.C. 124 Brigade and reported at YORK TRENCH at 8.0.p.m.
It was subdivided by Brigade orders into 2 half sections, one half section under Lieut. Hunter was ordered to report to the O.C. 26th Royal Fusiliers, and the other half under Sergt. Mossman was ordered to report to the O.C. 32nd Royal Fusiliers, both in EDGE TRENCH.
The section then proceeded to EDGE TRENCH, and finding no one there, went on to GREEN TRENCH, where they waited till 5.0.a.m. until the infantry arrived. The first battalion to arrive was the 26th Royal Fusiliers, and Lieut. Hunter accompanied them with 14 men.

Sergt. Mossman was left in GREEN TRENCH with the remaining
14 men , and accompanied a party of the 15th Hants, who
appeared in GREEN TRENCH, in accordance with the order of the
officer with the party, as far as SWITCH TRENCH, where he
reported to the O.C. 15th Hants, who ordered him to put in
two machine gun emplacements and a fire step in the trench.
This wasdone with infantry assistance.  On reporting completion
of the work to Col. Cary Barnard, he was ordered to return and
report to his Company.  This he did at 1.30.p.m. on the 15th..
Lieut. Hunter in the meantime reported to Col. North the O.C.
26th Royal Fusiliers, and assisted the infantry in consolidating
in SWITCH TRENCH.  On completion, the O.C. 26th Royal Fusiliers
ordered him to return, and he reported to the Brigade Headquarters
in YORK TRENCH, who said they had no further orders.  He
accordingly reported to the O.C. 237th Field Co. R.E. at 4.0.p.m.
on the 15th.

One section of the 233rd Field Coy. R.E. was ordered to
report at POMMIERS REDOUBT at 8.0.p.m. to the G.O.C. 123rd
Infantry Brigade, and Lieut. Langdale, who was in command,
received instructions to report to the O.C. 10th R.W.Kents.
The section bivouaced with the R.W.Kents till 12.30.a.m. on
the 15th, when the party moved from YORK TRENCH, arriving there
at 3.30.a.m.
No further instructions were received till 12.15.p.m. when the
battalion moved to the junction of MILK LANE and CARLTON TRENCH,
when they waited till 2.30.p.m. when the section received orders
to advance between "B" and "C" Companies and consolidate in
SWITCH TRENCH.   The section advanced among the various parties
of the R.W.Kents, and reached TEA TRENCH at about S.11.a.4.4.
Lieut. Langdale then reported to O.C. Battalion, who appeared
to be under the impression he had reached SWITCH TRENCH.
Lieut. Langdale then carried out a reconnaissance with a
section sergeant as far as SWITCH TRENCH, and sent back the
sergeant as a guide for the O.C. Battalion, who brought up a
part of his battalion and the sappers to SWITCH TRENCH.
At about S.5.a.7.2. Col. Woodmartin, who had given intructions
to a part of his battalion to move to the right about 800
yards and was then about to recall parties who had straggled
further off towards HIGH WOOD was wounded; by the time Lieut.
Langdale and one private had bound him up, all the infantry
had disappeared.  Lieut. Langdale then went to the forward
dressing station at S.11.c.0.5. and sent up a stretcher for
him.   Lieut. Langdale then turned up towards SWITCH TRENCH
and rendez-voused his sappers at the junction of MILK LANE
and CARLTON TRENCH reporting to Capt. Thwaites on his
arrival at about 7.0.p.m. on the 15th, who then took charge
of the halfsection with the other two sections that he was
taking up for consolidating work in rear of FLERS.   In the
meantime Crpl. Rice with half a section had moved with the
right column of the 10th R.W.Kents, and assisted the infantry
in consolidation of a portion of SWITCH TRENCH on the West of
the LONGUEVAL - FLERS Road.
At about 9.0.p.m. the work in hand was completed and no officer
being present, Corpl. Rice returned with his sappers to Company
Headquarters and reported himself.


The remainder of the R.E. acted under Divisional orders
conveyed through the C.R.E. on the night of 15/16th.
Capt. Baker was ordered to proceed with the remaining 3 sections
of his Company, 2 sectionsof the 237th Field Company and

one section of the 233rd Company to consolidate the line BOX - COX - HOGSHEAD in front of FLERS.

In front of LONGUEVAL, Capt. Baker and Lieut. Berry were severely wounded and Capt. Matheson took command of the six sections.

Information being received that no line in front of FLERS was held, Capt. Matheson then reconnoitred to ascertain where the front line was. Finding that the infantry had fallen back from HOGSHEAD and that the front line was on the right of FLERS from N.31.c.8.8. to N.31.d.6.6. he consolidated this line, making Strong Points on each flank, and one central one with also a machine gun emplacement on the right return flank. The work being completed at about 1.0.a.m. One section of the 237th Company and one section of the 233rd Company were left to consolidate in the BROWN LINE in accordance with instructions. Two sections of the 233rd Company, under command of Capt. Thwaites were employed at the same time consolidating behind the line of FLERS TRENCH behind FLERS. In continuation of the work carried out by Lieut. Carter in the day time using the old wire of FLERS TRENCH as an obstacle.

On the 16th the two sections who had not yet been employed worked on the improvement of the MONTAUBAN - QUARRY Road which was being used for evacuation of the wounded from the advanced dressing station.

On the night of the 16/17th four sections under command of Capt. Thwaites were ordered to proceed to FLERS to report to the commandant of FLERS.(Major OTTER) and consolidated the line BOX - COX - HOGSHEAD. Finding BOX occupied by the troops of the New Zealand Division, work was concentrated on COX and HOGSHEAD, and on completing the gaps in a connecting trench, which the infantry had dug, also in making a short length of C.T. back to the SUNKEN ROAD. The two sections at work in the BROWN LINE were ordered to be relieved and one additional section was sent to the GREEN LINE to work till 4.0.a.m. On the 17th these sections were again employed on the MONTAUBAN - QUARRY Road.

On the afternoon of the 17th all the Companies were withdrawn to camp at FRICOURT.

The lessons learned as regards R.E. Work are:-

1. That R.E. should as far as possible be employed under the direct orders of the Division on definite work of tactical value. The sections given to the brigades were left almost entirely on their own initiative without any definite instruction

2. No party of R.E. of less size than a section under an officer should be employed, except perhaps a few guides who would be very useful to show the infantry the way, and avoid the confusion which occurred through the lack of knowledge of the trenches and of the direction of the attack. These should rejoin their sections at once.

3. A preliminary engineer reconnaissance of the positions to be consolidated before the night parties of R.E. are sent out, would be very helpful in deciding what number of men, tools and materials are likely to be required.

4. One stretcher per R.E. Section should be carried. the Regimental stretcher bearer system is very apt to leave out the R.E. who have no stretcher bearers of their own. If two stretcher bearers per section could be added supernumerary to the strength, they would be very useful in other ways.

5. For tool transport, the pack cobs were found very useful, the conditons were impossibel for getting tool carts forward. This suggested that a second pack saddle per section should be carried for us on a spare horse or cob. This would enable one pick and shovel for each man to be carried so that the sappers could each carry up 25 sandbags for consolidation work.
In only one case was an infantry carrying party provided, and so that the sappers had to rely on what they could bring or find themselves.

6. Generally, the infantry do not appear yet to appreciate the tactical value of the sappers; and except where they were employed directly under Divisional orders with a Company Commander incharge, their work was apt to be misdirected. Probably, therefore, in working with a new army, especially as the junior or temporary R.E. officers are apt themselves to be lacking in Military experience, it is best to work the Field Companies, as far as possible, as complete units.

                          (Signed) E.N.Stockley,
                            Lieut. Col. R.E.
20.9.16.                    C.R.E. 41st Division.

# WAR DIARY or INTELLIGENCE SUMMARY

Vol 6   Army Form C. 2118

HQRs 41st Div. R.E. Brigades

October 1916

| Place | Date | Hour | Summary of Events and Information | Remarks and references to Appendices |
|---|---|---|---|---|
| RIBEMONT | 1st | | CRE with MAJr RNG reconnoitred the water supply of the villages of FLERS and SSAltr Sites for forward dumps. Also sites for two advanced Brigade HQrs. | |
| FRICOURT CHATEAU | 3rd | | CRE 41st Divn relieved CRE N. Zealand Divn of charge of Engineer work on the sector FRICOURT - L'MS BOYE (inclusive) to FLERS - LIGNY road. CRE moved to FRICOURT CHATEAU. The 3 Field Coys were in bivouac near MONTAUBAN. HQRE moved to FRICOURT CHATEAU. On the night of the 3rd/4th Oct. a Section of the 228 F. Coy RE with 2Coys 19th N.Sea. Pioneers and Corps Pon-trs-, 1/2 Coy 19th N.Sea & Machine gun Section all under command of Capt Moore, proceeded to carry out a chain of strong points in front of the front line with the object of fuck MS5t, on the old German strong point at M19b.5.8. on the FLERS LIGNY road, with the Ibn Rifleman of Salvd'r. This line across to the fortissimont Point held on the forD SUPPORT LINE at M24b.8.6. and was Carry off an outward renown in our line – About 300 yards on the rising the line with part of two CTs (one of back to the British front line was completed. The Advanced work taken up on the 3rd Octbr was the Commencement of two Class A Advanced Brigade Heads at M30c35.1 and M36b.4.7. Sites of these for closing up a gallery 30'x 5'x6' with 20ft of head cover are apparent. My Horse slipped burg. staff 3 – | |

# WAR DIARY or INTELLIGENCE SUMMARY

Army Form C. 2118

2nd Sheet

Oct 1916  HdQrs 13 Battalion

| Place | Date | Hour | Summary of Events and Information | Remarks and references to Appendices |
|---|---|---|---|---|
| FRICOURT CHATEAU | 3rd | | Beauville Street & Cow Lane (a Ry N.S.) and side roads from LONGUEVAL 2 Thro N Hand and from LONGUEVAL to NORTH STREET to the division of FLERS. The Trolleys in FLERS and well as FACTORY CORNER have been put and windlasses repaired and damage by shells repaired. Road repair had also been taken with infantry working parties in the LONGUEVAL & HIGHWOOD and LONGUEVAL NORTH STREET roads. The PIONEERS were employed on the four main communication trenches, TURK LANE – GOOSE ALLEY – PIONEER LANE – PINKLEY and in carrying on the Corps buried cable line towards FACTORY CORNER and a survey upon the SWITCH TRENCH. | |
| | 4th | | On the Right of H.S.L. 2 sections of the 237th F.C. under Capl Malcolm carried on work on the forward front line. Detns from it to the twenty front line – and 2 sections of the 223rd F.C. Coy Carried on Avy 300x assembly trench 150x & the line of the front line of the Left section. LIEUT. F. STURTON LANGDALE was killed this night whilst working in the Bde sector of M366.c.7. | |
| | 5th | | On the Right H.S. to 223rd F.C. Coy under Capt Thwaites proceeded 2 sections of H 232 F.C. Coy under Capt Thwaites proceeded to carry on the work on the forward front line on the Right & one section of the 228 F.C.Coy Carried on the work in the assembly trench in the Left sector. | |

# WAR DIARY or INTELLIGENCE SUMMARY

Army Form C. 2118

3rd Sheet

Oct 1916    H.Q. 151st Div. Inf. W.I.S.S.

| Place | Date | Hour | Summary of Events and Information | Remarks and references to Appendices |
|---|---|---|---|---|
| FRICOURT CHATEAU | 6th | | On the 6th October 1st Section C 228th 9th Coy under 2nd Lieut Kenyon moved ahead for operations on 7th Each to 722nd 9th Coy B.C. and 1 section of the 237th R.E. Coy under 2nd Lt Stratton with the 724th 9th Coy B.C. on tonight 6/7th. 2nd Lieut Stratton's section proceeded with Infantry Linking Party to complete the forward tramline to the right sector. | |
| | 7th | | During the operation on the 7th October, 2nd Lt Kenyon's section carried and commenced a strong point on the front line gained in the infantry attack. 2nd Lieut Kenyon was severely wounded and Sergt Grant took command. But Lieut Stratton's party was spare at the sub-sections, and only my Coy Hd Quar. 2nd Corpl S.T. Smith succeeded in carrying up a strong point on which the other Sub-section with 2nd Lieut Stratton Supply men was found. The other subsecn with 2nd Lieut Stratton Support Rear. Casualties and wounded to carry away work. The Consolidation parties in the right by 6 pm 7/8th consisted of 1 section of 228th 9th Coy under Lieut Hans and 2 sections of the 233rd R.E. Coy under Capt Fielding for the left and right Brigade sections of the front line respectively. On the left of the Consolidation party Completed the Strong Point Commenced by Kenyon's Section and extended it to the GIVENE. | |

1875 Wt. W593/826 1,000,000 4/15 J.B.C. & A. A.D.S.S./Forms/C. 2118.

# WAR DIARY or INTELLIGENCE SUMMARY

Army Form C. 2118

4th Sheet
HQrs 14th Div R.E.
Oct 1916

| Place | Date | Hour | Summary of Events and Information | Remarks and references to Appendices |
|---|---|---|---|---|
| FRICOURT CHATEAU | 7 | | On the right the Consolidation party consisted 550 yards of the new front line and dug 280 yards of C.T.s: this work was done with the assistance of Pioneers and Infantry. The remainder of the Pioneers were kept available for Constructing the four main C.T.s from front to rear and the keys of N. Staines. Pioneers Continued the Carrying forward of R.E. Stores to ASHALLEY and GOOSE ALLEY. | |
| | 8 | | On the night of 8/9 Oct a Consolidation Party Consisting of 1 Section of Each F. Coy. all under the Command of Capt Prevall, proceeded to the front line and the Pioneers was available as on the previous days & Carry on the Communication Trenches. | |
| | 9 | | On the 9th the Field Coys were allotted to Brigades areas for the Carrying out of a general defence and Reastering of Each Field Coy worked on the Right of 9/10 2nd Section 228th F. Coy in RESCUE BEETLE Communicated & STING POSN in the FAT Trench Line 2nd Section 233rd F Coy in the Reft BEETLE CR SIGNSIDE 160 yds of the front Line. 2nd Section 237 F Coy in the RegtL BEETLE as Complete respective HQ and 2/Lt Trench C.T. | |
| | 10 | 6.45 am | On the 10th Oct at 4.40 the R.E. Pioneers of H.Q. Divn commenced to Correspond end of the 305 F.E. | |
| BURE | 11 | | HQ. R.E. moved with Div HQ to BURE CAMP | |
| | 13 | | Field Coys & Pioneers were employed under orders of the CXV Corps forward to MONTAUBAN - BAZENTIN - LONGUEVAL - BERNAFAY WOOD road | |

**Army Form C. 2118**

5th Sheet

# WAR DIARY or INTELLIGENCE SUMMARY

HQ 1st Divn RE

OCT 1916

(Erase heading not required.)

| Place | Date | Hour | Summary of Events and Information | Remarks and references to Appendices |
|---|---|---|---|---|
| HALLEBAST | 16 | | 2/1stR2 move back from BOURG to THAZIER COURT. | |
| | 18th | | CRE left Hallebast for HAZEBROUCK en route for RENINGHELST to take over from CRE 4th Australian Divn | |
| FLETRE | 19th | | 2/1stR2 move by train from Pont-Remy to GODEWAERSVELDE for FLETRE | |
| RENINGHELST | 7th | | R.E. H.Q R.2 move to RENINGHELST. | |
| | 20th | | Command passed to HQ 1st Div 12 noon — | |
| | | | Disposition of R.E. Cos | |
| | | | 22 8th Fd Coy Billiard Midsham G36a.5.7. | |
| | | | 23 8th Fd Coy HQ R2 Midsham G36a.6.6. } R. Officer came to R.O | |
| | | | 2 Secs Spoilbank I33a.5.1 } Truck | |
| | | | 2 Secs Birchshot H30 c.6.7 | |
| | | | 237 Fd Coy HQ R2 Midsham G36a.7.8 } Inriyd/secn P.O Bruck | |
| | | | 3 Secs Hallebast N36.a.3 to VIERSTRAAT road - | |
| | 28th | | Lieut Met & R.2 T.R was appted acting Bde Major 123rd Infy Bde - 2/Lieut K.H. Smith 233rd Fd Coy (rivu as acting Adjt RE 1st Divn) | |

1-11-16 -

Mockley Lieut GCRE CRE 1st Divn

41 Div.
G.43.
67/20.

REPORT ON THE R.E. OPERATIONS 3RD TO 10TH OCTOBER, 1916.

On the 3rd October the R.E. were disposed as under:-

In bivouac near MONTAUBAN.
    228th Field Coy. R.E.        Capt. E.Moore, R.E. (S.R.)
    233rd Field Coy. R.E.        Capt. H.F.O.Thwaites, R.E.
    237th Field Coy. R.E.        Capt. C.L.T.Matheson, R.E.

Charge of the Engineer work in the sector between EAUCOURT L'ABBAYE exclusive and the FLERS LIGNY Road was taken over from the New Zealand Engineers at 4.p.m. on the 3rd October, and two companies of the 11th South Lancs (Pioneers) were placed under C.R.E. 41st Division, as well as the 19th Bn. Middlesex Regt. (Pioneers). On the night of the 3/4th - Two sections of the 228th Field Coy. with two Companies 19th Bn. Middlesex Regt. and ½ Company with Machine Gun section as covering party, all under the command of Capt. E.Moore, proceeded to carry out a chain of strong points, with its right flank resting in the old German Strong Point at M.19.b.5.8. on the FLERS LIGNY Road held by the 12th Division, and with the intention of extending this line across to the GIRD SUPPORT TRENCH at M.24.b.6.6. and thus cutting off an awkward reentrant in our line. Owing to difficult of access due to infantry reliefs, only a small proportion of the Pioneers followed up the Sappers, and consequently only about 300 yards of this line could be carried out with part of two C.T's leading back towards the existing front line.

On the 3rd October the R.E.commenced work on the two new tunnelled Brigade Headquarters at M.30.c.3½.½. and M.36.b.4.7. and carried on continuous reliefs on both these works until they were completed on the 9th October.
The other work taken up was road repair from LONGUEVAL to HIGH WOOD and the Decauville lines from LONGUEVAL to HIGH WOOD and LONGUEVAL NORTH STREET.
The 7 wells in FLERS and 1 well at FACTORY CORNER were taken over and windlasses refixed and damage by shelling repaired.
The Pioneers were employed on carrying in the Corps Buried Cable line towards FACTORY CORNER, and constructing a Survey Observation Post on the SWITCH LINE with tunnelled dugout.
The communication trenches were allotted to:-
    1 Company 19th. Bn. Middlesex to TURK LANE
    1 Company 11th Bn.South Lancs.to GOOSE ALLEY.
    1 Company 19th.Bn.Middlesex. to PIONEER LANE.
    1 Company 11th Bn. South Lancs.to FISH ALLEY.
and progress on all of these was carried on continuously when no other operations were in hand.
Some improvements were also made to the Adv. Bde. H.Q. at S.6.a.8.' and the Advanced Dressing Station at S.6.a.5.5.

On the night of the 4/5th October, 2 sections of the 237th Field Coy. under Capt. Matheson with 1 Company of the 26th Bn. Royal Fusiliers and 1 Company of the 32nd Bn. Royal Fusiliers proceeded to carry on the work in the forward front line. Only 1 officer and 11 men of the 32nd Bn. Royal Fusiliers followed the sappers up, and the result was that the only work that could be done was to spitlock out the line across the reentrant, and improve the work done the previous night and the forward C.T's.

Another party of 2 sections of the 228th Field Coy. under Lieut. Carter with 2 Companies of infantry detailed by the 122nd. Infantry Brigade laid out and dug 300 yards of assembly trench about 150 yards behind the front line to the West of GOOSE ALLEY.

On the night of the 5/6th, 2 sections of the 233rd Field Coy. under Capt. Thwaites with the same working party of infantry as had been detailed the night before, proceeded to complete the forward front line trench, difficulty was again experienced in reaching the line and no work was accomplished.
Another party of 2 sections of the 228th Field Coy. with 2 Companies 18th Bn. K.R.R. carried on the assembly trench on the left and completed the line as far as M.23.b.7.3.

On the 6th October, 1 section of the 228th Field Coy. under 2/Lieut. Kenyon was detached for operations with the 122nd Brigade and 1 section of the 237th Field Coy. under 2/Lieut. Stratton was detached for operations with the 124th Brigade. The remainder of the R.E. and Pioneers with the exception of the parties carrying on the Brigade Headquarters, the Survey Observation Post and the Corps Cable Trench were detailed to be in readiness in reserve from zero hour on the 7th October.

On the night of the 6/7th 2/Lieut. Stratton's section was detailed with an infantry working party to complete the forward front line, and succeeded in doing so.

During the operations on the 7th October, 2/Lieut. Kenyon's section laid out and commenced a strong point at about M.24.a.7.6. at about 8.p.m. they were driven back and held the former front line till 10.45.p.m.
2/Lieut. Stratton's section was split up under Brigade orders into two sub-sections; one of these under 2/corpl. S.J.Smith advanced with the fourth wave of the 21st.Bn.K.R.R. and constructed a Strong Point in the new front line in which the infantry were then forming; the other sub-section under 2/Lieut. Stratton advanced with the second wave of the 32nd. Bn. Royal Fusiliers, and reached a point about 250 yards in front of our line. The shelling and enemy machine gun fire was too heavy to allow of any work being done and after suffering heavy casualties the remainder of the section withdrew after daybreak.

On the night of the 7/8th October consolidation parties consisting of 2 sections of the 228th Field Coy. under Lieut. Alms and 2 sections of the 233rd Field Coy. under Capt. Fielding were detailed for the left and right Brigade sectors respectively to report at Advanced Brigade Headquarters for working parties.
On the left the consolidation party completed the Strong Point commenced by 2/Lieut. Kenyon's section and extended it to the GIRD LINE.
On the right the consolidation party connected 550 yards of the new front line and dug 260 yards of C.T's; this work was done with the assistance of Pioneers and Infantry.
The remainder of the Pioneers had been detailed for connecting the four main C.T's from front to back, and the 2 Companies of 11th.Bn.South Lancs Pioneers continued the carrying forward of FISH ALLEY and GOOSE ALLEY.

On the night of the 8/9th October a consolidation party consisting of 1 section of each Field Company, all under the command of Capt. Thwaites, proceeded to the front line and the Pioneers were detailed as on the previous night to carry on the communication trenches, but owing to infantry reliefs and difficulty of access little work was actually accomplished.

On the 9th October the Field Companies were allotted to Brigade areas for the carrying out of a defence scheme, the 228th Field Coy. in Reserve Brigade area commenced a Strong Point on the FAT TRENCH line on the night of the 9/10th, the 233rd Field Coy. in the left Brigade area consolidated 160 yards of front line on the night of the 9/10th, the 237th Field Coy. in the Right Brigade area completed and deepened 400 yards of C.T. from the front line.
Other work on the Defence Scheme was organised with the Infantry Brigadiers, and the Pioneers carried on work improving the communication trenches .

On the 10th October at 4.p.m. the R.E. and Pioneers were relieved by the corresponding units of the 30th Division.

14.10.16.                                    Lieut - Col. R.E.
                                             C.R.E. 41st Division.

41st Divisional Engineers.                    From 31st August 1916
                                                to 17th October 1916

## OPERATIONS ON THE SOMME.

### TOTAL WASTAGE OF PERSONNEL

| UNIT              | OFFICERS | O.R. |
|-------------------|----------|------|
| Headquarters R.E. | nil      | 1    |
| 228th Field Coy.  | 4        | 41   |
| 233rd Field Coy.  | 1        | 21   |
| 237th Field Coy.  | nil      | 17   |
| TOTAL             | 5        | 80   |

1/11/16

## 1st Divisional Engineers

**CASUALTIES INCURRED DURING OPERATIONS ON THE SOMME.** from 31st Aug. 1916 (date of last compilation) to 17th October 1916

| COMPANY | NATURE OF CASUALTY | OFFICERS | OTHER RANKS |
|---|---|---|---|
| 228th Field Coy. R.E. | KILLED | NIL | 1 |
| | DIED OF WOUNDS | | nil |
| | WOUNDED | Captain E.C. BAKER | 35 |
| | WOUNDED SLIGHT AT DUTY | Lieutenant T.B.BERRY II/Lt.H.A.KENYON | 2 |
| | WOUNDED AND MISSING | NIL | 2 |
| | MISSING | NIL | 1 |
| | MISSING BELIEVED KILLED | NIL | NIL |
| | ACCIDENTALLY WOUNDED | NIL | NIL |
| | EVACUATED SICK | Lieutenant E.T.G.CARTER (sprained ankle) | 4 |
| 233rd Field Coy. R.E. | KILLED | Lieut.E.F.J.STOURTON-LANGDALE | 2 |
| | WOUNDED | NIL | 11 |
| | WOUNDED SLIGHT AT DUTY | (Captain H.F.O.THWAITES, Lt.N.D.R.HUNTER & ( Lt.E.F.J.STOURTON-LANGDALE. | 4 |
| | WOUNDED AND MISSING | Nil | Nil |
| | Missing | NIL | NIL |
| | MISSING BELIEVED KILLED | NIL | NIL |
| | ACCIDENTALLY WOUNDED | NIL | 4 (3 evacuated) |
| | EVACUATED SICK | NIL | 5 |
| 237th Field Coy. R.E. | KILLED | NIL | 3 |
| | WOUNDED | NIL | 12 |
| | WOUNDED SLIGHT AT DUTY | NIL | 2 |
| | EVACUATED SICK | NIL | 2 |
| Hd.qtrs.R.E. | WOUNDED ACCIDENTALLY | NIL | 1 |

OPERATION ORDER NO.49/2, BY LIEUT.COL. E N.STOCKLEY.

C.R.E. 41ST. DIVISION.

Copy No. 2

1. The 228th, 233rd, 237th Field Companies, 19th Middlesex Pioneers, and 2 Companies 11th South Lancs. Pioneers, will be disposed as under during the next 24 hours.

   (a) The sections R.E. detailed below under Capt. H.F.O. THWAITES R.E. will consolidate Strong Points along the whole of the new 41st Div. front line. Capt. THWAITES will report to Brigade Headquarters at S.6.a.8.7. at 4.0.p.m. and ask for a working party if any available from the 122 and 124 Brigades, who should still be there at that time.

   The R.E. Sections viz:-

O.C. Capt. H.F.O. THWAITES.
   1 section 228th Field Coy. R.E.
   1 section 233rd Field Coy. R.E.
   2 sections 237th Field Coy. R.E.

   will report to Brigade Headquarters at S.6.a.8.7. at 5.p.m.

   (b) Remaining detail of R.E..

228th Field Coy.
   ½ section - Water supply in FLERS.
   2½ sections - Reserve in bivouac.

233rd Field Coy.
   2 sections - Continuous work Brigade Headquarters M.36.b.4.7..
   1 section - Reserve in bivouac.

237th Field Coy.
   2 sections - Continuous work Brigade Headquarters M.30.c.3½.½.

   (c) Detail 19th Middlesex Pioneers.
   100 men per Company to work on the same Communication trenches as last night, viz:- TURK LANE, GOOSE ALLEY, PIONEER LANE, FISH ALLEY. The work to be continued from front to rear as previously.
   One officer from each Company to report to Brigade Headquarters at S.6.a.8.7. at 5.p.m. for guides, and the Companies to report at the same place at 6.p.m., and to start work at 8.p.m.
   The work on Survey O.P. and Corps Cable Trench will be carried on in reliefs at as full a speed as remainder of men available permit.

   (d) Two Companies of 11th Battn. South Lancs. less 2 platoons will carry forward FISH and GOOSE ALLEYS as last night.
   2 Platoons 11th Bn. South Lancs. as in my R.E.263 clearing TURK LANE and FISH ALLEY from ABBEY ROAD to the rear.

2. Troops mentioned in para. 1(a) and the 100 men from each Company 19th Middlesex Pioneers as mentioned in para. 1(c) will cease work and withdraw one hour before dawn.

2.

3. For information that the 123rd Infantry Brigade will probably relieve 122nd Infantry Brigade on the night of 8/9th. Dividing line being about N. and S. Line between M.24 and N.19 between 123rd and 124th Brigades.

4. Acknowledge.

Copy No.1 to  41st Div. C.
     2.     122nd Inf. Bde.  by D R 12.15pm
     3.     123rd Inf. Bde.
     4.     124th Inf. Bde.
     5.     228th Field Coy.
     6.     233rd Field Coy.
     7.     237th Field Coy.
     8.     19th Middlesex.
     9.     11th South Lancs.
    10.     File.

8th October, 1916.

Lieut. R.E.
Adjutant for
C.R.E. 41st Division

# WAR DIARY or INTELLIGENCE SUMMARY

Army Form C. 2118

Nov 1916    HQrs 41st Divl Engineers

| Place | Date | Hour | Summary of Events and Information | Remarks and references to Appendices |
|---|---|---|---|---|
| RENINGHELST | 2nd | | Lieut G.C.E.N STOKER R.E. proceeded to THEZELE as acting C.E. & S.Corps — | |
| | | | Capt. H.F.O. THWAITES R.E. took over duty as acting CRE 41st Divn. | |
| | 1st | | 2nd Lieut J. Taylor joined 233rd Fld Coy R.E. | |
| | 4th | | | |
| | 6th | | Lieut. M.D.R. Hunter joined 47th Division as acting Adjt R.E. | |
| | 8th | | 2 Sections 233rd Fd Coy were flooded out of their Billets at DICKEBUSCH LAKE & moved to Billets in DICKEBUSCH G.33.B.8.8.. The flood also affected Divisional Headquarters at RENINGHELST & two found necessary to blow up the dams across the GROOTEBECK to save QHA from being swamped | |
| | | | The undermentioned N.C.O & Sappers were awarded Military Medals for gallantry on the SOMME. | |
| | | | N° 104 330 Sgt. E. GRANT 228th Fd Coy R.E. | |
| | | | N° 108 567 Sgt. A.J. WHITE 233rd Fd Coy R.E. | |
| | | | N° 108 517 Sgt. W. HAY 233rd Fd Coy R.E. | |
| | | | N° 108 568 Sapper F. MARSHALL 233rd Fd Coy R.E. | |
| | 10th | | Lieut. G.A. HARRIS R.E. joined 233rd Fd Coy R.E. from 42nd AT G R.E. | |
| | 12th | | Lieut. C.E. FISCHER R.E. joined 233rd Fd Coy R.E. from Base | |
| | 14th | | The 228th Field Coy R.E. relieved the 233rd Fd Coy R.E. in the Left — | |
| | 17th | | Sector of the front area & the 233rd took new work in the Back area | |
| | 23rd 24th | | from the 227th Fd Coy relieving Section by Section. Change of works joined from respective O.C.'s T.P. on 24/11/16 | |

# WAR DIARY
## or
## INTELLIGENCE SUMMARY
*(Erase heading not required.)*

Army Form C. 2118

| Place | Date | Hour | Summary of Events and Information | Remarks and references to Appendices |
|---|---|---|---|---|
| | 27th | | Lieut E.E. MARIETTE was Struck to the 2.3.7 K5 Ttd by Tel for a month when new duties posted to a Field by 2nd MARIETTE joined from the 23rd Pontoon Park | |
| | 28th | | Lieut F.F.R. PERKINS Adjutant 14/1st Divisional Engrs was appointed Adjutant Brigade vice 103rd Infantry Brigade with temporary rank of Captain. Captain PERKINS assumed his new duties on 30/11/16 | |
| | | | During the month, the two Field Cos in the forward area were engaged in the reclamation of the Reserve line, attn provision of a trench lewis with dugouts (but to knd the Reserve line, assistance being also given to the Infantry in the reclamation of the front line. ECLUSE TRENCH was also repaired & dugouts provided Also a Tunnel traced off it. The 1/5th Middlesex Reg.t (Pioneers) were employed on the improvement, widening & drainage of the front the Communication Trenches & also on the general drainage of the front area & the reconstruction of the trench Tramway system. In the back area, one Field Coy was employed in improving the huts accommodation established for the Infantry Brigades and considerable progress was made in this respect at MICMAC, OHIPPEWA, ONTARIO & ALBERTA Camps. | |

4/12/16

Ken R.O. Stewart
Lt.Col
O/C CRE 4 1st Division

ORDERS BY C.R.E.D/41ST DIVISION. 19 - 11 - 1916.

1. The 228th Field Company R.E. will relieve the 233rd Field Company R.E. in the forward area on the left sector, and the 233rd Field Company R.E. will take over the back area work from the 228th Field Company R.E. during the period.

2. The reliefs will be by sections and will take place after work each day.

   one section on 22.11.16.
      "     "    " 23.11.16.
      "     "    " 24.11.16.
      "     "    " 25.11.16.

3. Charge of R.E. work in respective areas will pass from the O.C's Field Companies concerned at 7.0.p.m. on 24.11.16.

4. O.C. 233rd Field Company R.E. will arrange for guides to lead the sections of the 228th Field Company R.E. up to their forward billets.

5. Section Officers with proportion of N.C.O's will reconnoitre their new work previous to taking over under arrangements that have already been made between O.C.'s 228th and 233rd Field Companies R.E.

6. acknowledge.

(Signed) H.F.O. THWAITES, Capt. R.E.

A/C.R.E. 41st Division.

Copy No. 1.  File.
         2.  War Diary.
         3.  41st Div. "G".
         4.  41st Div. "A".
         5.  122nd Inf. Bde.
         6.  123rd Inf. Bde.
         7.  C.R.A.
         8.  228th Field Coy. R.E.
         9.  233rd Field Coy. R.E.
        10.  Area Commandant.

**WAR DIARY** — ORIGINAL

**INTELLIGENCE SUMMARY** — December 1916

Army Form C. 2118

Vol 8

| Place | Date | Hour | Summary of Events and Information | Remarks and references to Appendices |
|---|---|---|---|---|
| RENINGHELST H'ts | | | Lieut Col E.N. STOCKLEY RE returned from leave and took over duties of CRE from Capt Trevallis who reported to 238th Fd Coy. | |
| | 25th | | Lieut J.H. SMITH proceeded on leave and Lieut J.F.H. Mews took over the duties of acting adjutant. | |
| | 26/27 & 14th | | 233rd Fd Coy relieved 228th Fd Coy in Left Sector. Officers Commanding Fd Coys were Promoted to rank of acting Major | CRO 1990 dated 14 Dec |
| | | | Major J.H.F.O. Thwaites M.C. RE 233rd Fd Coy. Major C.T. Mathieson M.C. RE 237th Fd Coy. Major F. Moore M.C. RE (SR) 228th Fd Coy. | |
| | | | During the month of Dec the progress of works on the Front was continued. | |
| | | | Right Sector — Reclamation of Present line and supervision Fren wire dumps 237th Fd Coy. — assistance to Infantry in reclamation & repair of front line. — Artillery OPs — Signal shell proof dugout. Road. B.A.P. Viersraat | |
| | | | Left Sector — Reclamation of Present line and repair of dugouts, communication 228th & 233rd Fd Coy — assistance to Infantry in reclamation front line. — Mg emplacements in Bus House — Yorkshire Balk St R's & M.G. Bayers. | |
| | | | Reserve Company 228th 233rd Fd Coy — Anti-aircraft platforms normans with Hutting work — | |

S.H.Stockley Lieut Colonel
CRE 41st Divn
2.1.17

**"A" Form.** Army Form C. 2121.

## MESSAGES AND SIGNALS.

| Prefix | Code | m. | Words | Charge | This message is on a/c of: | Recd. at | m |
|---|---|---|---|---|---|---|---|
| Office of Origin and Service Instructions. | | | Sent At | m. | Service | Date From | |
| | | | To By | | (Signature of "Franking Officer.") | By | |

TO — DAG.
3rd Echelon
Base.

| Sender's Number. | Day of Month | In reply to Number | | AAA |
|---|---|---|---|---|
| | 2nd | | | |

Herewith War Diary of this
Unit for the month of
May 1916.

R W Baker
Capt RE.

O/C 228TH (FIELD) COMPANY,
ROYAL ENGINEERS (BARNSLEY).

From
Place
Time

Original

Army Form C. 2118

# WAR DIARY
## or
## INTELLIGENCE SUMMARY

(Erase heading not required.)

HQ's 41st Divn. R.E.

JANUARY 1917

Vol 9

Instructions regarding War Diaries and Intelligence Summaries are contained in F.S. Regs., Part II. and the Staff Manual respectively. Title Pages will be prepared in manuscript.

| Place | Date | Hour | Summary of Events and Information | Remarks and references to Appendices |
|---|---|---|---|---|
| RENINGHELST. | 1st | | Major H.F.O. THWAITES. M.C. R.E., 233rd Fld. Coy. R.E. proceeded to course for R.E. Coy. Commanders at R.E. School of Instruction. G.H.Q. | |
| | 4th | | Lieut. N.D.R. HUNTER M.C. R.E. assumed the duties of Adjutant, R.E. on his return from leave. Lieut. G.F.H. ALMS R.E. returned to duty with 228th Fld. Coy. R.E. | |
| | 10th | | Major H.F.O. THWAITES. M.C. R.E. returned from School of Instruction. G.H.Q. | |
| | 12th | | 1/Lieut. J.W. SMITH. R.E. joined 237th Fld. Coy. R.E. | |
| | 19th | | 1/Lieut. R.H. CHAPMAN. R.E. left 237th Fld. Coy. R.E. on posting to 2nd Field Survey Coy. R.E. | |
| | 20th | | Major C.T.L. MATHESON. M.C. R.E. proceeded to course for R.E. Coy. Commanders at R.E. School of Instruction. G.H.Q. | |
| | 22nd | | Lieut-Colonel E.N. STOCKLEY. D.S.O. R.E., C.R.E. proceeded to England on 3 weeks leave, Major H.F.O. THWAITES took over the duties of C.R.E. during his absence. | |
| | 26/27 | | The 228th Fld. Coy. R.E. relieved the 233rd Fld. Coy. R.E. in the left sector of the Divisional front line & the 233rd Fld. Coy. R.E. took over the Hutting work in the rear area. | |

# WAR DIARY
## or
## INTELLIGENCE SUMMARY

Army Form C. 2118

(Erase heading not required.)

| Place | Date | Hour | Summary of Events and Information | Remarks and references to Appendices |
|---|---|---|---|---|
| RENINGHELST | | | During the month of January, the programme of works on the front line was continued. | |
| | | | R.F.W. Sector - Reclamation of Reserve Line and supervision trench walk dugouts carried out by Infantry in relaxation & training of front line. Augmented machine gun covers & extra O.P.s & sig. & tel. proof dugouts. New R.V.P. at VIERSTRAAT. | |
| | | | Left Sector - Reclamation of Reserve line and revision of dugouts, similar to 228th & 233rd R.E.Cys. Infantry in relaxation & front line. Work in S. Replacements in OUR HOUSE, OOSTHOEK FARM, VOORMEZEELE & the SPOIL BANK. Canada dugouts for M.G. and VOORMEZEELE area, Md. Res. | |
| | | | Reserve Company - Progress was continued in the provision of Materials & Stables 228th & 233rd MCs & Soldiers club at RENINGHELST was started in hand for the Division. | |

1.2.17.

[signature]
a/CRE 41st Division

**WAR DIARY** or **INTELLIGENCE SUMMARY**

Army Form C. 2118 — ORIGINAL

Hd Qrs. 41st Divisional Engineers Vol 10

FEBRUARY 1917

| Place | Date | Hour | Summary of Events and Information | Remarks and references to Appendices |
|---|---|---|---|---|
| RENINGHELST | 1st | | Major E. MOORE, M.C. R.E. proceeded to Course of Instruction for R.E. Coy Commanders at R.E. School of Instruction G.H.Q. | |
| | 3rd | | Capt. J.H. LANGTON R.E. 237 Fld Coy. R.E. left to take up the post of 2nd in Command of the 4th Battn. Royal Welsh Fusiliers. | |
| | 8th | | 2nd Lieut J. Fry 228' Fd. Coy. with 1 NCO and 3 Sappers took part in a raid on our Enemy's trenches and carried out demolition work. 12 prisoners were taken. 2nd Lieut J. Fry and 2nd Corpl P. Wilkinson were recommended for gallantry in this occasion. | |
| | 13 | | Lieut F.K. Scott joined the 237' F.Coy. — Lieut Col E. STOCKER, R.E. returned from leave and took over duty as C.R.E. | |
| | 24 | | 2nd Lieut E.L. 237' F.Coy with 2 N.C.O.s Sappers took part in a raid on the Hollandscher Beemst with the 10th Bn. Queen's West Surrey Regt and carried out demolition work. 65 prisoners were taken. R.E. casualties 1 NCO killed 7 sappers wounded — Lieut J.K. Scott R.E. was killed and the 2 sappers were killed in moving whilst laying out a tape for stretcher bearers from the front line to the VIERSTRAAT road. — 2nd Lieut Roberts, Lt. Col George (since upon the killed) and Sapper Pigott were recommended for gallantry on this occasion. | |

Army Form C. 2118

# WAR DIARY
## or
## INTELLIGENCE SUMMARY
(Erase heading not required.)

HQ 41st Div¹ Engineers.

FEBRUARY 1st 1917

Instructions regarding War Diaries and Intelligence Summaries are contained in F. S. Regs., Part II. and the Staff Manual respectively. Title Pages will be prepared in manuscript.

| Place | Date | Hour | Summary of Events and Information | Remarks and references to Appendices |
|---|---|---|---|---|
| RENINGHELST | | | During the month of February work on the front was continued, the main items being the construction of concrete dug-outs for Spr M.G. emplacements and the completion of certain concrete M.G. emplacements. Concrete O.P's and Signal Dug-outs are also being constructed. Concrete work was unavoidably delayed by the frost during the earlier part of the month. Progress hindered by weather conditions has been made in the reclaiming general improvement of the front and "R" lines, and a good deal of new fire stepping has been put in. The new R.A.P. at NIERSTRAAT and the Corps O.P. at CARRÉ FARM have been completed.<br><br>In the Reserve Area hutting and erabling was continued, but has been hampered for want of material. The Divisional Soldiers' Club at RENINGHELST is now nearly completed, a Canteen, and a Tea & Supper Room having already been opened.<br><br>3-3-16 | |

S M Mockler
Lieut Col R E
CRE 41st Div

Army Form C. 2118

ORIGINAL

# WAR DIARY
## or
## INTELLIGENCE SUMMARY

(Erase heading not required.)

HEADQRS. 185TH DIV. R.E.

MARCH 1917

No XI

Instructions regarding War Diaries and Intelligence Summaries are contained in F. S. Regs., Part II. and the Staff Manual respectively. Title Pages will be prepared in manuscript.

| Place | Date | Hour | Summary of Events and Information | Remarks and references to Appendices |
|---|---|---|---|---|
| RENINGHELST | 8th | | Lieut. K.H. Smith transferred from 233rd 2nd Coy to the office of A.D.R. 2nd Army and was replaced by 2nd Lieut. H.D. Dickman who joined 14/3/17 | |
| | 10th | | 2nd Lieut. F. L. Roberts transferred from 237 R.Coy to the 13th Railway Operating Coy and was replaced by 2nd Lieut. Rex Taylor – who joined 20/3/17 | |
| | 19th | | Capt. O. Mulloy, R.A.M.C. M.O.R.E. transferred to 735 Field Ambulance and was replaced by Capt. E. Ashby R.A.M.C. | |
| | 21st | | Capt. H.Z.B. Fielding transferred from 233rd F.Coy to command the 63rd Field Coy and was replaced by Capt. J.A. Anson. R.E. (S.R.) | |
| | 25th | | The Divisional sector R.A.E. Vierstraat has however now to be a brigade of the 75th Div. The 237' F.Coy. R.E. and advanced billets at HALLEBAST and moved to augment in F.M.R2 area near SCOTTISHWOOD. | |
| | 1st | | The organization of R.E. work was in preparation for the 75th Div. much with a view to increase of work in the forward area. All divisional F.Coys were given a sector of the line. Heavy 3rd section forward, and a section training and Whiskey Corps for the section relief, was arranged & troop shelter. | |

1875  Wt. W593/826  1,000,000  4/15  J.B.C. & A.   A.D.S.S./Forms/C. 2118.

**Army Form C. 2118**

# WAR DIARY
## or
## INTELLIGENCE SUMMARY

(Erase heading not required.)

MARCH 1917   172 RE 41 DIV.

| Place | Date | Hour | Summary of Events and Information | Remarks and references to Appendices |
|---|---|---|---|---|
| RENINGHELST | 1st | | The hutting work was arranged for by the formation of a Company's hutting party. Consisting of 2 R.E. Officers, 36 R.E. and 72 Infantry drawn equally from each R.E. Company and Battalion. Work was continued during the month on defensive preparations particularly the completion of concrete dugouts for M.G. Emplacements — reinforced dugouts and emplacements to cover tops flanks from the BLUFF and SPOIL BANK SALIENTS, and construction of Forward and Improvement and strengthening the Reserve Line, and construction of Forming and Relaxation of the front Line. During the month a programme of work in connection with the proposed offensive operations was drawn up and discussed in detail by the three Companies and Pioneers. | |

2-4-17

J.M. Walker Lieut Colonel
CRE 41 Division

ORIGINAL

H.Qrs. 4th Army R.E.   Vol 12

# WAR DIARY
or
## INTELLIGENCE SUMMARY
(Erase heading not required.)

**APRIL 1917**

Army Form C. 2118

| Place | Date | Hour | Summary of Events and Information | Remarks and references to Appendices |
|---|---|---|---|---|
| RENINGHELST. | 1st. | | For work on the preparations of Companies in preparation for the proposed offensive the R.E. Field Companies and Pioneers were allotted work as under:— | |
| | | | 228th Field Coy. All work in the RESERVE BATTn. area including OPs mentioned dugout accommodation to tactr RESERVE BATTn. and accommodation for 2 Companies in the JHR + LIERS and 2 Companies about VOORMEZEELE. Extension of the water main. — Shell proof Signal Visual stas. Ammunition dumps &c. | |
| | | | 233rd Field Coy. All work in the SUPPORT BATTn. area (DIVIDED CAVALRY BATTn.) trenches O25 — O31. Including the reclamation of the "MUD PATCH" and gaps in sides & ends of it to form a continuous front line. Reclamation of the support line and intermediate CTs from the front line and back to enable disposing Reserve line which is to be relaid in as a C.T. to the left sector. — Two advanced RPPS. Accessory work in connection with support Battn. Juniville HQ. for Runners &c. addl accommodation in Reserve line. | |
| | | | 237 Field Coy. All work in the RIGHT BATTn. area (trenches O14 — O24.) including the improvement of the front line. Reclamation of support line and intermediate CTs. — Juniville HQ for 2nd/18th and accessory work. Two advanced RPPS. Continuation of improvement of and addit'nal accommodation in Reserve line — | |

# WAR DIARY
## or
## INTELLIGENCE SUMMARY

(Erase heading not required.)

APRIL 1917    H.Q. R.E. 41st DIV.

Army Form C. 2118

| Place | Date | Hour | Summary of Events and Information | Remarks and references to Appendices |
|---|---|---|---|---|
| RENINGHELST | 12. | | The Pioneer Battn. parts all work on the improvements and extension of Kippers main C.T.s and natural routes (1) MIDDLESEX LANE (2) VICTORIA STREET (3) CONVENT LANE (4) TRAMWAY TRACK. With 2 & 1/2 Coys Connection. GORDON STREET to join up MIDDLESEX LANE and CONVENT LANE and provide communication across between Brigade HQrs. Also the repair and widening of the main road CAFE BELGE — VOORMEZEELE — S.E. 101. The 1st Canadian Tunnelling Coy. carry on the tunnelling work of the left-Bde Battn HR also New Battalion Battle HR off SHELLEY LANE. The 2nd Tunnelling Section carry on the tunnelling work of the Reserve Battn. Battle HR. The Field Companys forward Drills were rearranged to better suit the Reorganization of work and to put the Companies into their respective Battle Dispositions — By:— 228th Field Coy at DICKEBUSCH with Div. Reconnoit. Section attached in GHQ 2 line at I.30a.28. 233. Field Coy in GHQ line near KRUISTRAAT HOEK at I.36.b.9.9. 237. Field Coy at SHQ 2 line near SCOTTISH WOOD at I.35.d.5.6. Each Brigade is arranging to attack 1 platoon from each Battn. of the Bde to the Field Coys to live at forward Drills with the Field Coy and work with them on the preparation of work. These attached infantry to then in turn with the Field Coy during operations and form the carrying and working party with the R.E. | |

# WAR DIARY or INTELLIGENCE SUMMARY

Army Form C. 2118

(Erase heading not required.)

HEAD Q.RS 41ST DIVN R.E.

APRIL 1917

| Place | Date | Hour | Summary of Events and Information | Remarks and references to Appendices |
|---|---|---|---|---|
| RENINGHELST | 4. | | Forward billets of 237th F.Coy were moved to fields near DICKEBUSCH (H33-c-3-8) on account of repeated Shelling of SCOTTISHWOOD. | |
| | 23. | | Sites were selected for 5 Heavy Trench Mortar Emplacements and the construction of these was put in charge of 228th F.Coy. | |
| | 25. | | 2nd Lieut T.O. Frank 237th F.Coy was appointed to command the 196th Land Drainage Coy and promoted Acting Captain : being replaced on 30.4.17 by 2nd Lt. C.S.V. Cooke. | |
| | 30. | | Owing to repeated Shelling of the area about the R.E Field Coy billets at OUDERDOM it was decided to move the H.Qrs & workshop Lines to ROZENHIL Camp. This move was carried out on 1st May at R.E. Billets were being :— | |
| | | | 228th Field Coy. H.Qrs & Workshop Lines   ROZENHIL M6a 9.5   Forward billets DICKEBUSCH H34a 4.8 | |
| | | | 233. "     —    ROZENHIL M6a 7.6.    —    B.H.Q2 Wks H36.5.9.9. |
| | | | 237. "     —    ROZENHIL M6a 10.4.    —    DICKEBUSCH H33c3.8 |

S.M Hooley Lieut Col RE
CRE 41st Divn

3.5.17.

**WAR DIARY or INTELLIGENCE SUMMARY**

Army Form C. 2118

ORIGINAL

H.Q. 41st DIVN RE.

MAY 1917

Vol 13

| Place | Date | Hour | Summary of Events and Information | Remarks and references to Appendices |
|---|---|---|---|---|
| RENINGHELST | 1st | | During the month the work on the programme of preparations for the offensive was continued. All available RE troops employed in forward area and infantry working parties increased. Billets & forward bivouacs received as anyone in 1st Army Area. | |
| | 6th | | 2nd Lieut A.H. Hewlin 237' Field Coy evacuated to Base Hospital. | |
| | 11th | | 2nd Lieut J. Taylor 233rd Fd Coy was wounded by M.G. fire whilst working on the Support Line reclamation and died of wounds 13-5-17 | |
| | 16th | | 2nd Lieut R.G. Roberts joins 233rd Fd Coy. | |
| | 31st | | Lieut N.D.R. Hewlen promoted Acting Captain (Adjutant) Whilst so employed with H.Q. Divnl RE dated 26 Nov 1916. | |

2-6-17

S. M. Crocker
Lieut Col RE
CRE 41 Divn

Army Form C. 2118

ORIGINAL

# WAR DIARY
## or
## INTELLIGENCE SUMMARY

(Erase heading not required.)

HQ. 41st Divn R.E.

June 1917

Vol 14

| Place | Date | Hour | Summary of Events and Information | Remarks and references to Appendices |
|---|---|---|---|---|
| RENINGHELST | 6th | | The R.E. with attached infantry and the Pioneers were withdrawn from work and proceeded during the night to forward bivouacs in the S.HQ.I line near KRUISSTRAATHOEK. One section and attached platoon 233rd Field Coy R.E. were attacked for work under Lieut Royal, with 123rd Inf Bde.; One section and attacked platoon under 2Lt C.S.V. Cooke with 124th Inf Bde. One section 183rd Tunnelling Coy. R.E. under Capt Hamilton R.E. assembled in QUEEN VICTORIA ST. Tunnels for work under D winion in locating and clearing captured enemy Dug-Outs. | |
| | 7th | | During the operation on the 7th & 8th June Lieut Royal's party laid out and dug down strong points on the recently captured enemy's SUPPORT LINE at 12.30. P.M. Lieut Royal returned to the Company Bivouac, reporting the way to 2/s. O.C. 12.30 Inf Bde. as ordered. 2/Lt Cooke's party went over behind the 32nd Infantry and plans fourteen bridges over the DIEPENDAELE BEEK to enable the infantry to cover. After the capture of the DAMM STRASSE they constructed two strong points in front of that line went forward and assisted in the consolidation of the BLACK LINE returning to Company Bivouac at 5.0. P.M. as ordered. 16.6.17. | |

| | Army Form C. 2118 |
|---|---|

# WAR DIARY
## or
## INTELLIGENCE SUMMARY
(Erase heading not required.)

June 1917.     H.Qrs 4th DIVN R.E.

| Place | Date | Hour | Summary of Events and Information | Remarks and references to Appendices |
|---|---|---|---|---|
| RENINGHELST | 7th | | At 10.30 a.m. the 2,178th Coy R.E. under Major E. Milne R.E. moved forward to construct a firmer line in front of the DAMMSTRASSE. Sections of the line were dug and wired with one strand wire, and the intervals were layed. The line was also wingtrampled. The company returned to their bivouacs at 9.30 P.M. During the work two ratters of the attached infantry was killed and when returning from the work 2nd Lt. W.C. Morris R.E. was wounded.<br><br>The 231st & 183rd Coy. R.E. and attached infantry, less one section, constructed a trunk transport tracks from VOORMEZEELE MOUND to DOME HOUSE, via PICCADILLY FARM and OATEN WOOD.<br><br>The Trunk transport Route from HEMELRYK CABARET to SHELLEY DUMP was extended to SHELLEY FARM by the 233rd Field Coy. R.E.<br><br>"A" Coy (Capt Solomon) 19th Bn MIDDLESEX carried forward CONVENT LANE across NO MAN'S LAND to form OAK AVENUE<br><br>"B" Coy (Capt Pratt) cleared QUEEN VICTORIA ST. and carried it some distance towards the GERMAN LINE.<br><br>"C" Coy (Capt Roberts) carried forward the ST. ELOI tram line and prepared forward alignment.<br><br>D Coy (Capt Roatfrey) repaired main road from BUS HOUSE to ST. ELOI<br><br>16.6.17 | |

# WAR DIARY
## or
## INTELLIGENCE SUMMARY

Army Form C. 2118

(Erase heading not required.) HQ. O.R.S. 4th DIVN. R.E.

June 1917

| Place | Date | Hour | Summary of Events and Information | Remarks and references to Appendices |
|---|---|---|---|---|
| RENINGHELST | 7th | | The section 183rd Tunnelling Coy had very little success in tunnelling for enemy Tunnellers digging. The 9th Battn Infantry taken under to O.S. dum R.E. stood by in readiness to construct forward saps watching points if necessary. | |
| | 8th | | 133rd & 161st Coy R.E. with attached infantry continued the consolidation of the RESERVE LINE (BLUE) in front of the DAMMSTRASSE. 228th Fd Coy. R.E. with attached infantry continued the PACK TRACK from SHELLEY DUMP to RUINED HOUSE. 237th Fd Coy. R.E. converted pack track from VOORMEZEELE MOUND to DOME HOUSE into a wheeled transport track. Pioneers continued work as allotted for 7th. | |
| | 9th | | Work as under 7th and 8th continued. | |
| | 10th | | Work continued as above. | |
| | 11th | | Work continued. Officers and N.C.O.'s 237th Fd Coy R.E. reconnoitred front line and arranged forward work with 12th Inf Bde. 16.5.17. | |

# WAR DIARY or INTELLIGENCE SUMMARY

**Army Form C. 2118**

June 1917.   Hd. Qrs. 41st Divn. R.E.

| Place | Date | Hour | Summary of Events and Information | Remarks and references to Appendices |
|---|---|---|---|---|
| RENINGHELST | 12th | | 228th Field Coy with attached infantry and 1/2 Dur. tunnelling lutton working on left forward area now from CANAL to OBLONY ALLEY. 233rd Fd. Coy., left rear area, including left overland track from HEMELYRK CABARET to RUINED FARM and neighbouring whole forward area. 237th Fd. Coy R.E. with attached infantry and 1/2 Dur tunnelling lution working on right forward area from OBLONY ALLEY to ESTAMINET, 19th Bn. Middlesex Regt. (Pioneers) Road, St. Eloi CROSS ROADS to RUINED FARM, 'A' Coy., EIKHOF FARM to O.4 a.4.3; 'B' Company, St Eloi to HIELE FARM and DAMM DUMP (O.9 & 7.3.) and thence circular route to EIK HOF FARM and OAK DUMP. 103rd Fd. Coy. R.E. – completing light Railway from VOORMEZEELE to SHELLEY FARM. 104th Fd. Coy. R.E. – water supply forward area from wells and springs. 129th Fd. Coy. R.E. – Right rear area, including improvement of siding back to DOME HOUSE and continuation to DAMM DUMP. 13th Btn. Shearwood trestles (Pioneers) – Roads and Tram line. 4th Btn. Royal Welsh Fusiliers (Pioneers) – Roads and light railways | 16.6.17 |

# WAR DIARY
## or
## INTELLIGENCE SUMMARY

Army Form C. 2118

Hdqrs. R.E. 41st DIVISION. June 1917

| Place | Date | Hour | Summary of Events and Information | Remarks and references to Appendices |
|---|---|---|---|---|
| RENINGHELST | 14a |  | During operations on night of June 14th the 128th Fd. Coy. R.E. under Major E. Moore M.C. R.E. assisted the 122nd Hy. Bde. in consolidating the new positions gained. Major Moore was wounded in the head by shrapnel. Capt. Amran. 233rd Fd. Coy R.E. appointed acting O.C. 228th Fd. Coy R.E. vice Major Moore. |  |
|  | 15a |  | R.E. and Pioneers 24th Division returned to 24th Division and one Field Coy R.E. and two companies Pioneers 47th Division were placed at the disposal of C.R.E. for work on roads and tramways. |  |
|  | 22nd |  | Headquarters 41st Division moved to WESTOUTRE owing to the shelling of RENINGHELST. |  |
| WESTOUTRE | 23rd |  | R.E. and Pioneers 47th Division withdrawn. |  |
|  | 24a |  | ii Lt. O.W. Campbell 128th Fd. Coy. R.E. was severely wounded during the shelling of his advanced billet and died of wounds during the night. |  |

Army Form C. 2118

# WAR DIARY
## or
## INTELLIGENCE SUMMARY

(Erase heading not required.)

June 1917     HQRS R.E. 41st DIVISION

| Place | Date | Hour | Summary of Events and Information | Remarks and references to Appendices |
|---|---|---|---|---|
| WESTOUTRE | 27th | | 228th Field Coy. R.E. relieved by 517th Field Coy. R.E. 47th Division at advanced billets and moved back to wagon lines. | |
| | 28th | | Captain Shaw 102nd Field Coy. R.E. reported for duty as O.C. 228th Field Coy. R.E. vice Major Moore. Capt Emson rejoined 233rd Field Coy. R.E. | |
| | 29th | | 228th Field Coy. R.E. moved back to rest billets in the BERTHEN AREA. 233rd Field Coy. R.E. relieved by the 520th Field Coy. R.E. 47th Division and moved back to transport lines. 237th Field Coy. R.E. relieved by the 518th Field Coy. R.E. 47th Division and moved back to transport lines. | |
| | 30th | | 233rd and 237th Field Companies R.E. moved back to rest billets in the BERTHEN AREA. | |

Army Form C. 2118

# WAR DIARY
## or
## INTELLIGENCE SUMMARY

(Erase heading not required.)

H.Q.R.S. R.E. 41st DIVISION

June 1917

Instructions regarding War Diaries and Intelligence Summaries are contained in F. S. Regs., Part II. and the Staff Manual respectively. Title Pages will be prepared in manuscript.

| Place | Date | Hour | Summary of Events and Information | Remarks and references to Appendices |
|---|---|---|---|---|
| WESTOUTRE | 30th | | The 19th Bn MIDDLESEX REGT (Pioneers) relieved by the 4th R.W. Fusiliers (Pioneers) 47th Division and moved back to transport lines. C.R.E 47th Division relieved C.R.E at WESTOUTRE. C.R.E. and Adjutant proceeded on leave to the United Kingdom. Major N.F.O. Thwaites R.E. acting for C.R.E. and 2nd Lt J.R. Stratton R.E. acting for Adjutant. Appendix is a special report on the R.E. operations on the 7th, 8th & 9th JUNE (BATTLE OF MESSINES) with map. Also a tabulated statement showing casualties and wastage during the 8 months continuous work in the line in the YPRES Salient. | |

SMPorter
Lieut Col R.E.
CRE 41st Divn

30-6-17

41st Div.
G.D.31.

Report on the R.E. and PIONEER Operations on 7th, 8th, and 9th June, 1917.
----------------------------------

On the night of the 6/7th the R.E. and PIONEERS were disposed as under in bivouacs and dugouts in G.H.Q.2.line between KRUISTRAATHOEK and VOORMEZEELE.

228th Field Coy. R.E. with attached Infantry and Divisional
Tunnelling Section.    -    Major E.MOORE,R.E. (S.R.)

233rd Field Coy. R.E. (less 1 section) with attached
Infantry.    -    Major H.F.O.THWAITES,R.E.

237th Field Coy. R.E. (less 1 section) with attached
Infantry.    -    Major C.L.T.MATHESON,R.E.

In G.H.Q.2.line between KRUISTRAATHOEK and ELZENWALLE.

19th Bn. Middlesex Regt.    -    Lieut-Col.A.I.IRONS.

One section 183rd Tunnelling Coy. R.E. was also placed at the disposal of the Division for locating and clearing tunnelled dugouts in the captured area and was quartered in the QUEEN VICTORIA STREET tunnels under command of Capt. HAMILTON,R.E. (T.C.)

One section of the 233rd Field Coy. R.E. under command of Lieut. H.M.BOYD,R.E. was detached for operations with the 123rd Infantry Brigade which attacked on the left of the front allotted to 41st Division.
Lieut.BOYD accompanied one of the infantry waves to the enemy's Support Line where he got into communication with the O.C. 20th Durham Light Infantry, with whom he selected and taped out four strong points.  He then sent a runner back for his section and attached platoon and constructed
(a) the four strong points shown on the map in blue.
This work was completed by 12.30.p.m.    The men being then exhausted Lieut.BOYD after making a further reconnaissance of the other more forward strong points decided to withdraw to the Company bivouac in accordance with his orders, reporting to the G.O.C. 123rd Infantry Brigade on his way down.

One section of the 237th Field Coy. R.E. under command of 2/Lieut. G.R.V.COOKE,R.E. was detached for operations with the 124th Infantry Brigade which attacked on the right of the front.  This section with their attached platoon of infantry went over behind the last wave of the 32nd Royal
(b) Fusiliers and placed fourteen bridges over the DIEPENDALE BEEK to enable the 26th Royal Fusiliers to advance on the DAMMSTRASSE ; they then went on to the DAMMSTRASSE and made
(c) two strong points in front of it, shown on map in blue.
When the infantry had reached the BLACK LINE they went forward and assisted in the consolidation of the front line and construction of Vickers Gun Emplacements at positions
(d) shown in blue.    The section withdrew as ordered on completion of this work and reported at Company bivouac at 5.0.p.m.

The principal duty allotted to the R.E. Field Companies on the 7th was the alignment and consolidation of a reserve line in front of the DAMSTRASSE.

This duty was allotted to Major E.MOORE,R.E. with the whole of his Company (228th Field Coy.) attached infantry and the Divisional Tunnelling Section.

The attack having been so successful the consolidation party moved forward at 10.30.a.m. instead of waiting for dusk and working till 8.0.p.m., arriving back at 9.30.p.m. The alignment laid out is shown in blue and this was kept well forward with the object of gaining a good field of fire and avoiding too close proximity to the DAMSTRASSE which appears likely to become a shell trap.

Sections of the line were dug and the connecting links taped out. The whole line was signboarded and a single barbed wire fence run along it.

On the 8th June the consolidation of this line was completed by the 253rd Field Coy.R.E. with attached infantry, and a 3 ft. trench dug to depth along the whole line. An apron fence of wire was put up to complete what had been done the previous day, and the Divisional Tunnelling Section was employed in putting in box dugouts.

On the 9th June the further improvement of the line and wire was carried out by the 237th Field Coy. R.E. with attached infantry and more dugouts added by the Divisional Tunnelling Section.

Two pack transport routes were laid out on the 7th instant in extension of the routes commenced previous to operations with the object of enabling transport to reach the line clear on either side of VOORMEZEELE.

The Right hand route from HALLEBAST, GORDON FARM, VOORMEZEELE MOUND was extended to PICCADILLY FARM, OATEN WOOD and DOME HOUSE and was laid out by the 237th Field Coy. R.E. picketed and bridged and made passable for pack transport by the night of the 7th : this route was improved on the 8th and used for wheeled transport taking up materials for consolidation on the 9th.(See yellow line on map).

The Left hand route from KEMMELRYK CABARET, ENGLISH WOOD, KRUISTRAATHOEK to SHELLEY DUMP was extended on the 7th to SHELLEY FARM as a passable route for wheeled transport and marked out to RUINED FARM for pack animals. This route was improved and carried forward by the 228th Field Coy. R.E. on the 8th and further improved by the 253rd Field Coy. R.E. on the 9th inst : a large number of fascines had to be got up to cross the boggy ground near SHELLEY FARM and the forward portion of this route is over exceptionally rough ground. (See yellow line on map).

The Pioneer Battn. was allotted work as under on the 7th :-

"A" Coy. (Capt. SOLOMON) carried forward CONVENT LANE across NO MAN'S LAND to join OAR AVENUE.

"B" Coy. (Capt. PRATT) cleared QUEEN VICTORIA STREET and carried it some distance across towards the German lines.

"C" Coy. (Capt. ROBERTS) carried forward the ST ELOI tram line from OXFORD STREET across the Reserve Line and prepared forward alignment.

"D" Coy. (Capt. GODFREY) repaired the main road from
BUS HOUSE to ST ELOI with a view to getting road material
forward for the making up of the road ST ELOI to BISHOP
FARM.
On the 8th it was decided not to continue the communication
trenches further and on the 8th and 9th "A" and "D" Coys.
worked on the main road ST ELOI to BISHOP FARM clearing
and making alignment across the crater area, and "B" and "C"
Coys. carried forward the ST ELOI tram line across NO MAN'S
LAND in the direction of DOME HOUSE keeping clear to the
West of the alignment of the ST ELOI - OOSTAVERNE road on
which the Pioneers of the 24th Division are working.

The section of the 182rd Tunnelling Coy. R.E. on the 7th
searched the captured area for mined dugouts and found
very little existing as the enemy appears mostly to have
built concrete blockhouses where a strong dugout was
required : a system of mined dugouts in the embankment
towards the West end of the DAMMSTRASSE is now being
explored and reclaimed with new entrances from the North
side for use as a Brigade Hd.Qrs.

The Hutting Section under Lieut. A.S.Glover, R.E. was
ordered to stand by on the 7th with preparations made
for moving forward horse watering points if it were decided
to move transport lines forward : as this was not done the
section did most valuable work in getting up stores to
VOORMEZEELE R.E. Dump and getting road material forward
to BUS HOUSE.
The VOORMEZEELE Dump is now well stocked, and a forward
dump at DOME HOUSE being formed.
SHELLEY Dump is also being shifted forward to RUINED FARM.

*[signature]*

Lieut. Col. R.E.

9.6.1917.  C.R.E. 41st Division.

# 141st INFANTRY BRIGADE.

## INTELLIGENCE REPORT
### CANAL & SPOIL BANK SUB-SECTORS
from 6 p.m. 31-5-17 to 6 p.m. 1-6-17.

**HOSTILE WORK.**

New sandbagging at O.3.d.54.95. and O.4.a.10.25.

**HOSTILE WIRE.**

A few new coils of barbed concertina wire have been thrown over and on parapet of IMPACT TRENCH at I.34.b.50.15. linking up two large patches of broken and tangled barbed wire.

**M.G. O.P. MINENWERFER ETC.**

M.G. at approx. I.34.c.95.13. active during the night.
Sniper active from position at I.34.d.35.93. Two box periscopes were in use to the right of this position.
Our snipers claim two hits.

**HOSTILE ARTILLERY.**

The RAVINE was shelled between 9.15 p.m. and 9.30 p.m.
At 10.20 p.m. enemy opened a barrage of 77 mm H.E. and shrapnel on area from RAVINE to SUNKEN ROAD. Barrage ceased at 10.40 p.m.
Occasional shells were fired on SPOIL BANK and RAVINE during the day.
In reply to our barrage at 3.30 p.m. enemy heavily shelled SPOIL BANK: BLUFF CRATERS: RENNIE AVENUE: RAVINE and our Supports and communication trenches both N. and S. of the Canal.
Intermittent shelling of RAILWAY DUGOUTS and SHRAPNEL CORNER during the day.
At 6 p.m. 1st inst, several 10.5 c.m. shrapnel fired over S.P.7 and WOODCOTE FARM.

**HOSTILE MOVEMENT.**

Enemy were seen running about in their support lines during our barrage this afternoon apparently endeavouring to escape the shelling.
Slight movement seen at gaps at I.34.d.35.93. and I.34.d.30.87.
A party of 21 men in fatigue dress and wearing shrapnel helmets were seen to hurry past gap in IMPERIAL SUPPORT at I.34.d.58.17. at 6.15 a.m.

**MISCELLANEOUS.**

Hostile aircraft very active and flying very low over our lines during the day.
An aeroplane passed over the BLUFF flying in an Easterly direction at 11.45 p.m.
At 9.55 p.m. 3 red lights were fired from behind enemy Lines.
At 10.45 p.m. signalling with a lamp was observed behind enemy's lines, opposite the RAVINE for 15 minutes. The following groups were read :- A.T.R.J.P. - KIM.K.O.T.
During our barrage this afternoon enemy sent up lights as
follows :-   3.32 p.m.   2 Red lights.
             3.40 p.m.   1 White light.
             3.45 p.m.   2 Red lights.
             3.48 p.m.   1 Red light.
6,000 rounds fired by our Vickers guns on enemy's works and communication.

Brigadier General,
Comdg. 141st Inf. Bde.

## 141st INFANTRY BRIGADE.

### INTELLIGENCE REPORT
### CANAL & SPOIL BANK SUB-SECTORS
from 6 p.m. 1-6-17 to 6 p.m. 2-6-17.

**HOSTILE WORK.**

Enemy appears to be making considerable efforts to repair his front and support lines South of the Canal as several working parties were seen during the night and early morning and were dispersed with L.G. fire. At 5 a.m. this morning a working party was observed working on OAK TRENCH AVENUE. Both rifle and Lewis Gun fire were opened on the party.

Many new sandbags at O.3.b.70.08. where a snipers post has been erected.

Two new hurdles have been placed across OAK SUPPORT at O.4.a.54.06.

**HOSTILE WIRE.**

Some of the gaps between O.3.b.90.02. to O.3.b.60.04. have been wired during the night.

New coil of concertina wire on parapet of IMPERIAL TRENCH at I.34.b.50.17. and a new coil in front of I.34.d.36.96.

**M.G. O.P. MINENWERFER ETC.**

Suspected O.P. at O.3.b.72.05. consisting of a large square box.

Enemy M.G's inactive during the night.

Between 12.30 a.m. and 3 a.m. about 50 Rifle Grenades were fired on our front line between NORFOLK ROAD and ESTAMINET LANE.

**HOSTILE ARTILLERY.**

Enemy artillery normal during the day.

Occasional rounds were fired on our Supports and Communication trenches N. and S. of the Canal during the day.

Enemy retaliated on the Western end of the SPOIL BANK in reply to our wire cutting.

**HOSTILE MOVEMENT.**

Movement observed at O.3.b.63.04. during the early morning.

Man seen running along trench at I.34.d.20.50.

At 10.15 a.m. 4 men were seen walking from WHITE CHATEAU (on top of trench) to O.4.d.10.81. where they disappeared.

Men were seen to run past gaps at I.34.d.36.95. and I.34.b.55.21.

A man carrying a square box on his head, size of box about one foot square with a handle on top, at I.34.d.50.65.

**MISCELLANEOUS.**

Transport heard during the night behind enemy's lines.

At 2.30 a.m. a fire was observed in enemy's lines about O.6.a.

Early this morning several explosions were heard behind enemy's lines.

Enemy airctaft very active during the day.

At 4.20 a.m. enemy aeroplane fired one white light followed by one red.

A single red light was fired from the enemy front line just South of the Canal. No action followed.

At 10 a.m. one of our planes landed between CHESTER FARM and HAZELBURY FARM, apparently owing to engine trouble, and ascended at 3 p.m. without mishap.

P.T.O.

MISCELLANEOUS. Contd.

At 12.10 a.m. enemy fired a double red light opposite the RAVINE in response to a hurricane burst of fire by our artillery. No action followed.

North of the Canal Enemy's Very Lights below normal and with only a few exceptions were fired obliquely into his front line from his Supports.

Several small fires were reported behind the enemy's lines during the night, probably dumps burning.

At 9.35 a.m. hostile balloon brought down in flames by one of our planes. Occupant descended in a parachute. Bearing 74° True from I.34.b.10.07.

J. Sheppard
Lieut. Intelligence Officer

for Brigadier General,
Comdg. 141st Inf. Bde.

2nd June 1917.

# 141st INFANTRY BRIGADE.

*War Diary*

### INTELLIGENCE REPORT
### CANAL & SPOIL BANK SUB-SECTOR
### from 6 p.m. 2-6-17 to 6 p.m. 3-6-17.

**HOSTILE WORK.**

Signs of new work on Sap at O.4.a.60.62.
Gap in trench at O.3.b.60.05. has been screened with hurdle revetment.
New brushwood revetting visible in IMPERIAL TRENCH at I.34.b.46.10.

**HOSTILE WIRE.**

About 20 yards of concertina wire has been put out at O.4.a.00.10.

**M.G. O.P. MINENWERFER ETC.**

O.P. and snipers post at O.3.b.80.08. has been destroyed by our T.M. fire.
20 rifle grenades were fired on front line S. of the Canal between 12.15 a.m. and 3 a.m.
A few trench mortars were fired by the enemy on the BLUFF SECTION between 6.30 p.m. and 7.30 p.m.
Snipers position at I.34.d.35.93. has been built.

**HOSTILE ARTILLERY.**

Report on retaliation for our bombardment between 3 p.m. and 3.30 p.m. forwarded separately.
Hostile artillery displayed greater activity during the past 24 hours.
Our front, Support and Reserve Lines, also SPOIL BANK were shelled during raids on right and left of Divisional front at 10 p.m. and 11.15 p.m.
Enemy retaliation consists mainly of isolated bursts of fire on our Support Lines, BLUFF and the SPOIL BANK.
Between 7.30 p.m. and 8.55 p.m. vicinity of BLAUWE POORT FARM heavily shelled with 15 c.m. H.E.
Intermittent shelling of the RAVINE and Supports during the day.

**HOSTILE MOVEMENT.**

Movement reported in enemy front line South of the Canal at "Stand to" this morning.
Movement observed in wood at O.4.a.9.2. at 4.30 a.m.
During our T.M. bombardment of Crater at O.4.a.85.80. at 11.45 a.m. a man wearing steel helmet was observed to jump out and run along trench.
Two of our 4.5" Hows. exploded in IMPERIAL TRENCH and 4 men were seen to run from vicinity of explosion to a dugout at I.34.d.32.75.
At 4.30 a.m. a man passing junction of IMPERIAL TRENCH and IMPUDENCE TRENCH was fired on and believed hit. Enemy retaliated by throwing three egg bombs in front of our parapet at top of HEDGE ROW.

**MISCELLANEOUS.**

During the night Very Lights were fired from Craters at O.4.a.85.80.
At the commencement of our demonstration shoot today a hostile balloon opposite our front was immediately lowered.
Hostile aircraft very active during the day.
Between 12.35 a.m. and 12.45 a.m. 19 double green lights were fired by the enemy just S. of the Canal. No apparent action followed.
Our snipers claim two hits.

**DAMAGE.** Our trenches in the RAVINE HAVE been damaged.

J. Sheppard
Lieut. Int. Officer
pp. Brig. Genl.
Comdg. 141st. Inf. B.

## 141st INFANTRY BRIGADE.

### INTELLIGENCE REPORT
### CANAL xxxxxxxxxx SUB-SECTORS
### from 6 p.m. 3-6-17 to 6 p.m. 4-6-17.

**HOSTILE WORK.**
    Nothing to report.

**HOSTILE WIRE.**
    Nothing to report.

**M.G. O.P. MINENWERFER ETC.**
    Minenwerfers fell in vicinity of BLUFF CRATERS at intervals between 6.30 a.m. and 7.30 a.m.

**HOSTILE ARTILLERY.**
    At 10.15 p.m. after our bombardment double green lights were fired by the enemy opposite the BLUFF CRATERS followed by double red lights. Enemy then shelled the Craters with 10.5 c.m. H.E.
    At intervals during the morning enemy shelled the BLUFF CRATERS: THAMES STREET and RENNIE AVENUE with 10.5 c.m. H.E.
    Between 2.45 a.m. and 3.45 a.m. enemy shelled BEDFORD HOUSE and vicinity with gas shells.
    BEDFORD HOUSE was shelled intermittently during the day becoming very heavy between 1.30 p.m. and 4 p.m.
    RAVINE and vicinity shelled intermittently throughout the day.
    Between 11.44 p.m. and 12.15 a.m. and 12.44 a.m. and 12.53 am enemy put up a barrage from on Supports and Reserves from SUNKEN ROAD to the RAVINE. Three batteries of four guns each firing on flash bearings of 124° T., 131° T. and 140½° T. from I.34.b.23.00.
    At 4.3 a.m. seven 10.5 c.m. H.E. shrapnel fired on CHESTER FARM.
    Between 6.45 a.m. and 7.10 a.m. enemy was apparently registering his front line and NO MAN'S LAND opposite RAVINE SECTOR. One battery only was firing.

**HOSTILE MOVEMENT.**
    Slight movement observed in enemy crater at O.4.a.82.81. at 4.30 a.m.
    At 5.30 a.m. three of the enemy were seen in front of "B" Crater wearing polished steel helmets, dark blue pleated coats and light coloured breeches. On being fired on they ran back to Crater at O.4.a.82.81. One man appeared to be wounded.
    At 6.45 a.m. an Officer wearing peaked cap came up communication trench at O.4.a.95.78. Shortly afterwards fire was opened on the Craters with 10.5 c.m. H.E. Fire was intermittent for 30 minutes and 2 guns were firing.
    2 men seen to pass gap at O.4.a.50.06. at 3.24 p.m.
    A few exposures were observed in IMPERIAL TRENCH: IMPERIAL AVENUE and IMPERIAL SUPPORT.

**MISCELLANEOUS.**
    Hostile aircraft very active during the past 24 hours in many cases flying low over our lines.
    3 Yellow Lights breaking into sprays were fired from IMPERIAL SUPPORT between 10.25 p.m. and 10.30 p.m. No apparent action followed.
    Very lights normal and fired from Support Lines.
    At 2.1 a.m. 4 golden rain lights from IMPERIAL SUPPORT at I.34.d.75.55. during rapid fire by our artillery.

Sheppard
Acting Intelligence Officer

Brigadier General,
Comdg. 141st Inf. Bde.

## 141st INFANTRY BRIGADE.

### INTELLIGENCE REPORT
from 6 p.m. 9-6-17 to 6 p.m. 10-6-17.

**HOSTILE WORK.**
Nil.

**HOSTILE WIRE.**
Nil.

**M.G.O.P. MINENWERFER ETC.**
Snipers have been less active during the past 24 hours.
A sniper was firing early this morning from an emplacement at approx. O.5.b.70.70. At 11 a.m. this emplacement was hit by one of our 4.5" Hows. Three men were seen struggling to free themselves from the debris and were fired at by our snipers.

**HOSTILE ARTILLERY.**
There has been an increase in the enemy's artillery fire during the past 24 hours. Several batteries firing from a N.E. direction.
Considerable attention was paid to our old system of trenches between the RAVINE and BLUFF.
Enemy's shooting was very erratic.
The Triangular Spoil Bank (O.5.a.) IMPERIAL LANE and OAF AVENUE was shelled intermittently during the day with 7.7 c.m. H.E. and shrapnel.
There was considerable shelling during the night of IMPUDENCE SUPPORT, IMPERIAL SUPPORT and communication trenches with 7.7 c.m. - 10.5 c.m. H.E. and shrapnel.

**HOSTILE MOVEMENT.**
Movement was observed in I.36.d. and O.6.b. chiefly in OAK KEEP and IMPERFECT TRENCH.
During the afternoon 3 parties of 10 men each were seen walking across the open at O.6.b.10.90. They were fired on by our 18-pdrs.
Much movement has been observed along road situated on the ridge at O.6.b. to O.6.d. and there appears to be many strong dugouts situated along the side of the road.
Movement also seen at Pioneer Park at approx. O.6.a.5.4.
A party of 7 men were seen walking along the Western side of Railway Cutting at approx. O.6.a.3.7.

**MISCELLANEOUS.**
Hostile aircraft fairly active.

Acting Intelligence Officer

Brigadier General,
Comdg. 141st Inf. Bde.

## 141st INFANTRY BRIGADE.

### INTELLIGENCE REPORT
from 6 p.m. 10-6-17 to 6 p.m. 11-6-17.

**HOSTILE WORK.**

There is a considerable amount of new work visible on OBLIQUE TRENCH.

**HOSTILE WIRE.**

New wire has been put out in front of building at O.5.c.75.15.

**M.G. O.P. MINENWERFER ETC.**

Enemy M.G's and Snipers inactive.

**HOSTILE ARTILLERY.**

Hostile artillery again active on our Supports, Reserves and Communication trenches.

BEIGE ROW and O.B.1. in vicinity was shelled at intervals during the day.

Enemy opened a heavy barrage on our front system at 10.30 pm lasting until 11.45 p.m. We replied with a very heavy counter barrage. During the barrage the enemy fired numerous red and green lights. From 2 a.m. to 4 a.m. enemy heavily shelled area O.4. and I.34.b and c. with H.E. and gas shells.

Hostile artillery was less active S. of the Canal during the day.

Intermittent shelling (at times becoming intense) of area I.34.b. and d. and I.35.a. and c. with H.E. and shrapnel throughout the day.

The following barrage lines were observed during enemy's bombardment last night -
1. From O.5.a.95.60. to I.35.c.70.10.
2. From QUARRY (O.5.a.45.95.) to S.E. corner of Triangular Spoil Bank (O.5.a.50.30.).
3. Along OAF DRIVE from O.5.a.0.4. to O.5.a.45.65.

The following True sound bearings were taken from O.5.a.50.45. -
1. A battery of 15 cm firing this morning on O.5.a. $104\frac{1}{2}°$.
2. Between 1.30 p.m. and 2 p.m. 2 batteries of 15 cm firing on BATTLE WOOD from $147°$ and $123°$.
3. At 11.38 a.m. 25 10.5 cm were fired on O.5.a. - $120°$.
4. A 7.7 cm battery was firing on a bearing of $94\frac{1}{2}°$ (sound and flash).

The following True sound bearings were taken from O.5.b.15.94. -
1. A battery of 4 guns 10.5 cm firing on BATTLE WOOD $86\frac{1}{2}°$.
2. One gun firing H.E. and shrapnel on IMPERIAL SUPPORT at half minute intervals $66°$. Time of report to burst of shell 9 seconds.
3. A/A gun firing on our aircraft $107\frac{1}{2}°$.
4. A battery of 4 10.5 cm firing on Battn. on Left $64°$.
5. One 10.5 cm gun firing on vicinity of IMPACT TERRACE $89°$. Time of report to burst 5 seconds.
6. One battery of 4 7.7 cm firing shrapnel in vicinity of WHITE CHATEAU on flash bearing of $125°$.
7. Four guns fired H.E. shrapnel in vicinity of OAF ROW on bearing $99\frac{1}{2}°$.

A true flash bearing of $154\frac{1}{2}°$ from I.34.d.67.75. was taken on heavy gun, probably 8", firing in direction of YPRES between 3.10 p.m. and 3.30 p.m.

/MOVEMENT.

- 2 -

HOSTILE MOVEMENT.

From 7 p.m. to 10 p.m. twenty parties of enemy (4 or 6 in each party) were seen walking up and down road at I.36.d.64.42. and on being fired at by our snipers and M.G's disappeared into trench which runs along or near the road. They were wearing shrapnel helmets and were without equipment or rifles.

At 2.30 p.m. party of 3 men walked along road at I.36.d.64.42. and at 2.35 p.m. a man was seen to run to a hedge at this point.

Movement was observed in OBLIQUE TRENCH and CAP KEEP.

MISCELLANEOUS.

Hostile aircraft was active during the day and at 6 p.m. (11th inst) 3 planes flew very low over the Canal about O.4.b.; the leading plane fired a reddish coloured light which was repeated when over THE STABLES. Ten minutes later the plane fired two more similar lights over the Canal and shortly afterwards hostile artillery fired 3 heavy shrapnel immediately over the broken bridge at O.4.b.2.5.

At 11.45 a.m. this morning six enemy planes came over our front, one flying at about 800 feet.

Several small dumps were exploded in enemy's lines during the night.

Between 4 a.m. and 5.30 a.m. 4 heavy explosions were heard and seen in village behind enemy's lines on a true bearing of 141½° from O.5.b.15.94.

At 12.5 p.m. an enemy plane fired at our men in Front and Support trenches with machine gun.

At 4.15 a.m. enemy transport wagon drawn by two horses passed along road at I.36.d.64.42.

Brigadier General,
Comdg. 141st Inf. Bde.

11th June 1917.

## 141st INFANTRY BRIGADE.

### INTELLIGENCE REPORT
from 6 p.m. 11-6-17 to 6 p.m. 12-6-17.

**HOSTILE WORK.**

The debris in front of entrance to dugout at O.6.b.81.92. has been cleared away.

**HOSTILE WIRE.**

No fresh wire reported.

**M.G. O.P. MINENWERFER ETC.**

A suspected sniper at O.5.d.10.50. was shelled by our 18-pdrs this morning.
Between 1 a.m. and 4 a.m. enemy machine guns were very inactive.

**HOSTILE ARTILLERY.**

Enemy artillery less active during the day.
Enemy shelled O.B.1 and 2 and O.C.1 and 2 during the night at intervals. The shelling was in the nature of short hurricane bursts of 10.5 and 15 c.m. H.E. and shrapnel.
During the morning enemy appeared to be registering on the road from O.5.b.50.90. to I.35.d.10.20. and occasional rounds were fired on our Supports and Reserves and in vicinity of BLUFF CRATERS.
The following true sound and flash bearings were taken from O.5.a.45.45. -
1. Between 10 p.m. and 11 p.m. flashes were observed at 45½°- 56½° - 75½° and 79½°. +62½°
2. A battery of 10.5 cm firing on BATTLE WOOD during the morning on sound bearing of 111° and 112½°.
3. A 15 cm gun firing on IMPULENCE SUPPORT and BLUFF sound bearing 90½°.
4. At 2 a.m. flashes observed from 107°, 111°, 105° and 96°.
The following true sound and flash bearings were taken from O.5.b.15.94. -
1. A single gun (10.5 cm) firing on vicinity of OAK LANE 519.
2. Gun firing shrapnel over OAK DRIVE from 111°.
3. A battery 10.5 cm firing shrapnel over BATTLE WOOD from 127½°.
4. Four guns 15 cm firing on BATTLE WOOD from 112°.
5. One 10.5 cm firing H.E.Shrapnel over junction of IMPERIAL SUPPORT and IMPERIAL SWITCH at intervals of four minutes on bearing of 112°. Time from report of gun to burst 7 seconds.
6 Several 10.5 cm fired into BATTLE WOOD from 66½°.
7. One 10.5 cm H.E. firing on IMPERIAL TRENCH from 75°.

**HOSTILE MOVEMENT.**

Between 4.20 a.m. and 4.50 a.m. men were seen frequently passing along road from O.6.b.82.60. to O.6.b.90.22.
Movement seen at entrance to dugout at O.6.b.81.92.
At 11.37 a.m. two men were seen walking from Railway towards SPOIL BANK (O.5.b.) and were fired on by our snipers and disappeared into some dead ground at O.5.b.91.72.
At 11.39 a.m. a man appeared at O.6.a.80.72. and crawled up Railway Embankment and disappeared over the embankment.

/VIS.

- 2 -

MISCELLANEOUS.

Hostile aircraft very active during evening and early morning.

Several loud explosions were heard and flames seen at 6.45 am this morning on true bearing of 97° from O.5.c.45.45.

Hostile Observation Balloons were observed on true bearings of 114°, 94°, 126°, 79° and 36½° from I.34.d.20.20.

Enemy very lights were sent up during the night from X.I.36.c.central.

Smoke was observed this morning at I.36.d.05.03. and I.36.d.65.15.

At 8.30 p.m. 2 hostile aeroplanes flew over our front line North of the Canal one of them dropping 2 red lights.

At 9.45 p.m. numerous RED and GOLDEN RAIN lights were sent up by the enemy opposite Battalion on left followed by a heavy bombardment with 10.5 cm and 15 cm on BATTLE WOOD. Our artillery retaliated at 9.50 p.m. and RED and GOLDEN RAIN lights were sent up from I.36.d.64.45. and gun opened fire on IMPERIAL LANE. Enemy's fire ceased at 10.30 p.m.

Very lights were fired from RAILWAY EMBANKMENT and near the Eastern end of the SPOIL BANK in O.5.b., three lights being fired before dark.

A small red paper balloon fell in our lines South of the Canal. It came from an Easterly direction.

At about 8.15 a.m. one of our planes fell in flames S.E. of WHITE CHATEAU.

Sheppard
Lieut. Intelligence Officer

Brigadier General,
Comdg. 141st Inf. Bde.

12th June 1917.

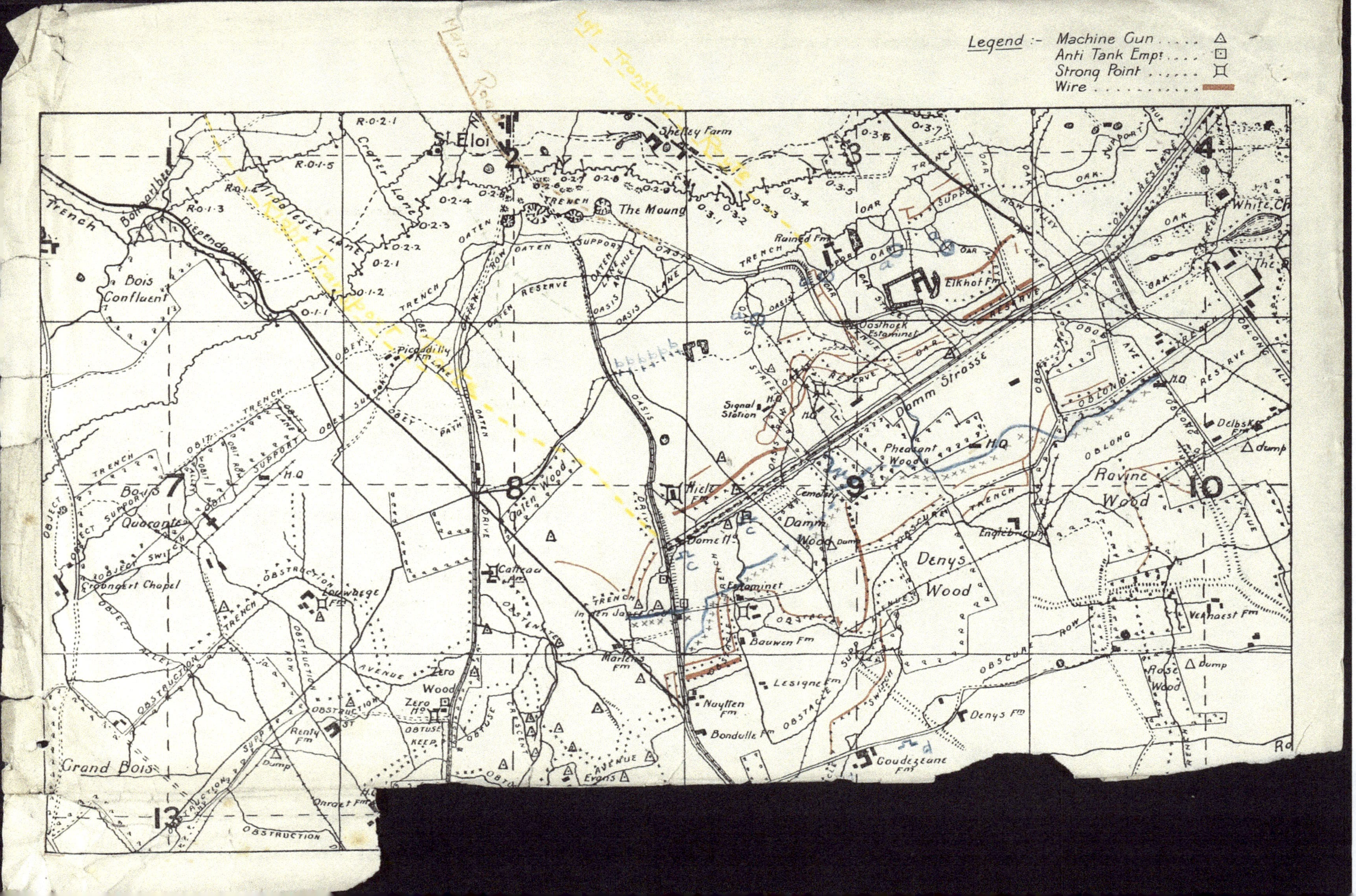

Message

..........DIVISION.
Map reference
or Mark on Map
at back.

1. My {Company / Platoon} has reached..............

2. My {Company / Platoon} is at.............. and is consolidating.

3. My {Company / Platoon} is at..............and has consolidated.

4. Am held up by M.G. at..............

5. I need :—Ammunition.
   Bombs.
   Rifle Grenades.
   Water.
   Very lights.
   Stokes shells.

6. Counter attack forming up at..............

7. I am in touch with..............on {Right / Left} at..............

8. I am not in touch with..............on {Right / Left}

9. I am being shelled from..............

10. I estimate my present strength at..............rifles.

11. Hostile {Battery / Machine Gun / Trench Mortar} active at..............

Time.......... m.   Name..............
Date..............   Platoon..............
                     Company..............
                     Battalion..............

3.

The section of the 1st Canadian Tunnelling Coy. R.E.
inspected the dugouts in the RED LINE, RAILWAY EMBANKMENT
and the cellars of HOLLEBEKE.
Four concrete dugouts were discovered in the RED LINE
in fair condition also several cellars in HOLLEBEKE
affording protection, but no tunnelled work was found.


Headquarters,
Royal Engineers,
41st Division.
Aug.4th, 1917.

Lieut. Colonel R.E.
C.R.E. 41st Division.

The work allotted to the 228th and 233rd Field Coys. R.E. for July 31st/Aug.1st was the consolidation and wiring of the RED LINE both North and South of the CANAL. The 228th Field Coy. R.E. South of the CANAL were successful in continuing a line of trench dug by the 11th Royal West Kents Regt. up the junction of our original front lines as shown in red on attached map. The original front line was wired and also the greater portion of the new trench. The Company also constructed a foot bridge across the canal at point "C"

The G.O.C. decided the situation North of the CANAL was not sufficiently clear to admit of further work on the night of July 31st/Aug.1st.
On the night of Aug.1/2nd the 233rd Field Coy. R.E. were able to improve a portion of the trenches dug the previous day to extend the line to tape out and wire same.
On the night Aug.2/3rd a further 200 yards was dug.
South of CANAL on the night of Aug.1/2nd a further 130 yards of RED LINE dug and another 100 yards of entanglement fixed, 56 yards of new Communication Trench dug and boarded and old Communication Trench improved.
On Aug.2/3rd Communication Trenches were further extended.

The 237th Field Coy. R.E. constructed a pontoon bridge across the CANAL on the night of July 31st. The detachment working under the command of 2/Lieut. TAYLOR R.E. formed up the bridge in 23 minutes. During the night three pontoons were damaged by shell fire; they were replaced and traffic was only delayed for 15 minutes. The Company has since maintained and guarded the bridge.
The remainder of the Company were employed in carrying forward the CANAL ROAD from the pontoon bridge towards BUFFS BANK. The approaches to bridges were well maintained and damage by shell fire repaired. A crossing for horse transport over the North side of CANAL banks near NORFOLK LOCK was commenced at 5.0.a.m. and was ready for use by 11.30.a.m.
Two footbridges were thrown across the CANAL as shown on map, one of which was destroyed by shell fire.
A signboard patrol fixed the notice boards required.
On the night of Aug.1/2nd work was carried on on the CANAL ROAD as far as weather conditions would permit, and the foot bridge across CANAL improved.
On Aug. 3rd. further work on roads and construction of bridge for Field Artillery over DIEPENDAAL BEEK at O.8.c.80.95.

19th Bn. Middlesex Regt.
The Pioneer work carried out by this Battn. was as follows:-
Night of July 31st/Aug.1st carrying forward OAF AVENUE from old front line; clearing OPTIC TRENCH and setting out forward work ; completing track South of CANAL and laying tramlines towards R.A.P. No.1. Work on road NORFOLK LOCK to RAVINE WOOD and the forward extension of CATERPILLAR TRACK as a pack route towards KLEIN ZILLEBEKE.
Aug.1/2nd. Continuation of above.
Aug.2/3rd. Continuation of above. Improvement and extension of Communication Trenches where weather conditions would permit.

/The.

REPORT ON THE R.E. AND PIONEER OPERATIONS ON
31ST JULY, 1ST & 2ND AUGUST, 1917.
------------------------------

On the night of the 30/31st July the R.E. and Pioneers
were disposed as under in dugouts and bivouacs: the Field
Companies R.E. in the vicinity of BOIS CARRE and the
Pioneers near VIERSTRAAT, all East of the VIERSTRAAT-
YPRES road.

228th Field Coy. R.E. (less 1 section) with attached
      Infantry. Major W.L.SHAW R.E. (T.C)

233rd Field Coy. R.E. (less 1 section) with attached
      Infantry. Major H.F.O.THWAITES R.E.

237th Field Coy. R.E. with attached infantry.
      Major C.L.F.MATHESON R.E.

19th Bn. Middlesex Regt.     Lieut. Col. A.I.IRONS

One section of the 1st Canadian Tunnelling Coy. R.E. was
also placed at the disposal of the Division for locating,
clearing and reinstating tunnelled dugouts in HOLLEBEKE
and the RAILWAY EMBANKMENT.

One section of the 228th Field Coy. R.E. with attached
platoon of 18th K.R.R.C. under command of Lieut. P.P. ADAIR R.E.
was detached for operations with the 122nd Infantry Brigade
which attacked on the right of the front allotted to the
41st Division. Lieut. ADAIR followed up the waves of
attacking infantry to a point beyond the enemy front line
and commenced to clear and reconstruct an old enemy
Communication Trench to extend the approach CAX AVENUE to
new front line. The work was carried on intermittently
owing to heavy shell fire.

No.2 Section of the 233rd Field Coy. R.E. with an attached
platoon of the 20th Durham Light Infantry under the command
of Capt. R.D.R. HUNTER, R.E. was detached for operations
with the 123rd Infantry Brigade carrying out the attack on
the left of the Divisional front. Capt. HUNTER followed
up the last wave of the 11th Queens Regt. to a line 100 yards
beyond the enemy front line. He commenced to tape out the
RED LINE beginning at the CANAL, but as the dugouts in the
CANAL and RAILWAY EMBANKMENT had not yet been mopped up
he laid out and had dug the line shown in red on attached
map. He then proceeded along the RED LINE and found that
parties of the 10th Royal West Kents and 20th Durham Light
Infantry had dug short lengths of line in the positions
shown respectively in blue and green on attached map.
All work was greatly hampered by hostile sniping, machine
gun and shell fire. Having incurred considerable casualties
and considering further work on the RED LINE inadvisable
by day, Capt. HUNTER withdrew his men at 10.0.a.m.
He reported the results of his work to the 123rd Infantry
Brigade.

       2.       /The

**Army Form C. 2118**

ORIGINAL

# WAR DIARY or INTELLIGENCE SUMMARY

(Erase heading not required)

**HQrs 41st DIVNL ENGINEERS.**

**JULY 1917**

Vol / 5

| Place | Date | Hour | Summary of Events and Information | Remarks and references to Appendices |
|---|---|---|---|---|
| near BERTHEN Sheet 27. R.21.a.28. | July 1st | | H.Q. R.E. moved into rest billets at marginally named place. Field Coys. started programme of training, including route marches, lectures and a practical "refresher" course. Sports were intended to be held by each company, the 233rd Coy. along too, the 9 Nick, but had to be abandoned by the others owing to future work. The attached Infantry Platoons remained with the Field Coys. during rest. | |
| | 11th | | 233rd Coy. R.E. and 2 Coys. Pioneers (19th Middlesex) placed at disposal of 47th Division to assist in preparations for coming operations. 233rd Coy. R.E. moved forward to camp in RIDGEWOOD A. to be within practicable distance of their work. They were employed on construction of transport track North of the Canal to serve Left sector in the offensive. 1 Section of 228th Coy. R.E. was attached to 233rd Coy. R.E. for this work. 237th Coy. R.E. and 2 Coys. 19th Middx. were put under C.E. II Corps for work on forward roads. | |
| | 12th | | 2 Sections 228th Coy. R.E. were sent to LUMBRES for work under 2nd Army. H.Q. & remaining Section 228th Coy. R.E. carried out work in training area, repairing ranges, marking out trenches for the practising of the coming attack, etc. | |
| | 18th | | In order to assist 47th Division in the stocking of dumps of R.E. material 2 Coys. S. Infantry from 123 Bde. were attached to 233rd Fd. Coy. Who took to hand the stocking of IMP DUMP, the Left Sector R.E. Dump, and a dump containing stores for immediate consolidation purposes i.e. wire, screw pickets & sandbags, at BUFFS BANK close up to the present front line. For some purpose 1 Coy. Infantry from 122 Bde. was attached to 228th Fd. Coy., whose H.Q. & remaining Section moved on this date to RIDGEWOOD Area. The | |

1875 Wt. W593/826 1,000,000 4/15 J.B.C. & A. A.D.S.S./Forms/C.2118.

# WAR DIARY
## or
## INTELLIGENCE SUMMARY

Army Form C. 2118

Hd Qrs 41st Divl Engineers     July 1917

| Place | Date | Hour | Summary of Events and Information | Remarks and references to Appendices |
|---|---|---|---|---|
| Near BERTHEN | July 16th | | 228th Fd Coy. took in hand the stocking of OAK DUMP, the Right Sector R.E. Dump, and a consolidation dump off OAK AVENUE C.T. close to its junction with the front line. | |
| | | 20th | 233rd Coy. R.E. started work on (1) extension of 4" pipe tramed along DAMMSTRASSE to proposed water point S.W. of WHITE CHATEAU. (2) Construction of approaches for pontoon bridge to carry guns over Canal & preparation for having all pontoon bridging equipment ready near the site for making the bridge one day before the attack. (3) Construction of steel girder bridge over NORFOLK LOCK at I 35.d.2.5. to provide for two way traffic passage of heavy guns across the Canal. | |
| | | | 1 Coy. 19th Middx. started laying tramline from SPOILBANK along southern bank of Canal at flow level, to cross Canal at IMP DUMP. This to provide for evacuation of wounded brought down to IMP DUMP from R.A.P.'s by high level tramline. Above work is nominally under C.E. II Corps but is Divisional. The conveyance of material from NORFOLK LOCK to IMP DUMP is being done by pontoon raft with sledges. The road on North Bank of Canal being still poor & frequently shelled at night, when only, owing to balloon observation, transport can proceed along it. Major A.G. Rainsford Hannay DSO. R.E. Egyptian Army (once for temporary attachment. | |
| | 21st | | R.E. and Pioneers at 41st Divn took over work in Divnl area from corresponding units of 47th Divn — | |

# WAR DIARY
## or
## INTELLIGENCE SUMMARY

(Erase heading not required.) H.Q. 41st DIVNL ENGINEERS

JULY 1917

Army Form C. 2118

| Place | Date | Hour | Summary of Events and Information | Remarks and references to Appendices |
|---|---|---|---|---|
| WESTOUTRE | 25 | 3 p.m. | 41st Divn took over Sector KLEIN ZILLEBEKE to HOLLEBEKE front from 47th Div. R.E. Pioneer work was arranged for as under:- | |
| | | | 228th Field Coy. All work in Brigades Sector South of Canal including working up the forward construction stores at Oak Dump and on Oak Avenue, rear front line. Improvement of Oak Dump Road and Cork Avenue. Improvements of tram line and Decca road from Stein Tunnel HOLLEBEKE. | |
| | | | 233rd Field Coy. All work in Brigade sector North of Canal including working up of the forward construction materials at Imp Dump and in BUFFS BANK rear front line. Improvement of the CATERPILLAR TRACK as a transport route from LOCHARELLE FARM thro' RAVINE WOOD to CATERPILLAR. Carrying on a trace along the Canal Bank Buffs Bank. Improving communication in the lower part and Impartial avenue. To | |
| | | | 237th Field Coy. Extension of the 7th trail-main along the Canal Bank Lock to DAMM STRASSE. Bridging NORDOCK LOCK with an infantry bridge and making approaches for guns & transport. Widening and improving the transport road along the North of the Canal from NORDOCK LOCK to IMP DUMP with the approach to SHREWSBURY NFY. the BLUFF CRATERS. Approaches to & siting causeways for a pontoon bridge at Okk 77. | |

**Army Form C. 2118**

# WAR DIARY or INTELLIGENCE SUMMARY

(Erase heading not required.)

HQ 1st DIVL ENGINEERS.

JULY 1917

| Place | Date | Hour | Summary of Events and Information | Remarks and references to Appendices |
|---|---|---|---|---|
| WESTOUTRE | 25 | | The 4/R.W. Middlesex Regt. (PIONEERS) was detailed for work as under:— | |
| | | | A Coy. — Improvement and extension of OAF AVENUE to front line N of CONVA. | |
| | | | B Coy. — Improvement and duckboarding of OPTIC AVENUE to front line Sth CANAL. | |
| | | | C Coy. — Tramline maintenance and continuing new line along Shirley canal from Norfolk lock to Coop Canal at Opp. 9.6 and track to kn Pilkin below MR. Dumps with extension via higher level from the Cliff above MR Dump P. Corner. | |
| | | | RAPS A℅ 1 + 2 | |
| | | | D Coy. — Maintenance Indicator of CATERPILLAR TRACK and branches to Norfolk lock Bridge but also to the BLUFF CRATERS. | |
| | 26. | | RE Field Coys Pioneers were Intraders at dusk to forward Machine between to BOIS CARRÉ and VIERSTRAAT. | |
| | | | Sec. 227 R.E. Construction of duck & Pontoon bridge of 72 ft Span (4 pontoons) across to canal at Opp. 7.7 to give an alternative route for the assault of the infantry for the attack. The reports Completion & the bridge was not at F.M.R. 10 A.m. | |
| | 27. | | The HISTORIC ATTACK was at 3.50 A.M. and comprised the line BECK FARM — HOLLEBEKE — GREEN BEG FARM. a report on RE operations will be attached to diary for AUGUST. | |

F. Mackay Lt. Col. R.E.
CRE 1st Div.

31-7-17

S E C R E T

O.C. 228th Field Coy. R.E.
O.C. 233rd Field Coy. R.E.
O.C. 237th Field Coy. R.E.
41st Div. "G".           )
41st Div. "Q".           )
C.R.A. 41st Divn.        ) For information.
122nd Infantry Brigade.  )
123rd Infantry Brigade.  )
124th Infantry Brigade.  )

----------------------

1. A pontoon bridge of 72 ft. span will be constructed by the 237th Field Coy. R.E. at dusk on Y/Z night at O.4.a.7.7. The approaches are already being constructed and camouflaged and the site chosen marked with small notice boards for guidance of any reconnoitring officers.

2. The bridge will carry infantry in fours and field guns: Infantry crossing the bridge must break step: horsed transport will proceed at a walk: no heavy guns may cross this bridge, but will cross by NORFOLK BRIDGE or at the BRICKSTACK.

3. The sloping banks of the canal are pitched with brick so that the Weldon trestles are not suitable for carrying the shore bays. The bridge will therefore be constructed with four pontoons.

4. O.C. 228th Field Coy. R.E. will place two pontoons with two bays of superstructure at disposal of 237th Field Coy. R.E.
O.C. 233rd Field Coy. R.E. will leave afloat his two pontoons as a standbye; these to be moored about the bend of the canal close to the South bank and camouflaged.

5. The bridge will be constructed by "forming up" from the South bank, no anchors will be used: pontoons will be moved alternately up and down stream to a cable laid across the canal.

6. All stores will be laid out previous to operations under the cliff at O.4.a.2.7. out of view of the enemy's balloon and camouflaged from aerial observation.

7. Completion of the bridge to be reported to C.R.E. and repeated C.R.A. through Battn. H.Q. at the South abutment of the IRON BRIDGE.

M Hickey

Lieut. Colonel R.E.
C.R.E. 41st Division.

23rd July, 1917.

# SECRET

123rd Infantry Brigade.
O.C. 233rd Field Coy. R.E. (For information).
-----------------------------

        Reference 41st Division Order No. 140 para 4, the section R.E. attached to your Brigade for the attack will be No. 2 section, 233rd Field Coy. R.E. under command of 2/Lieut. H.A. DICKMAN R.E. with a platoon under command of 2/Lieut. A.R. WILLIS 20th Battn. D.L.I. attached.

        Kindly issue any further detailed orders as to place of assembly and duty to be carried out to the Section Officer who will wait on you for instructions if you so desire.

                                                              *Stockley*

20th July 1917.                                           Lieut. Col. R.E.
                                                      C.R.E. 41st Division.

| | | | |
|---|---|---|---|
| Copy No. | 1. | 1st Canadian Tunnelling Coy. R.E. | |
| " " | 2. | 228th Field Coy. R.E. | |
| " " | 3. | 233rd Field Coy. R.E. | |
| " " | 4. | 237th Field Coy. R.E. | |
| " " | 5. | 19th Bn. Middlesex Regt. | |
| " " | 6. | 41st Division "G" (For information) | |
| " " | 7. | 41st Division "Q" | -do- |
| " " | 8. | 122nd Infantry Brigade | -do- |
| " " | 9. | 123rd Infantry Brigade. | -do- |
| " " | 10. | 124th Infantry Brigade. | -do- |
| " " | 11. | C.R.E. 24th Divn. | -do- |
| " " | 12. | C.R.E. 19th Divn. | -do- |
| " " | 13. | C.E. Xth Corps. | -do- |
| " " | 14. | C.R.E. 41st Divn. | |

SECRET.          COPY NO. 9          July 29th, 1917.

## 41ST DIVISIONAL ENGINEERS OPERATION ORDER NO. H.Z.2.

1. The 41st Division will attack on "Z" day in accordance with orders and instructions already issued.

2. Field Companies R.E. and Pioneers will rest on "Y" day in their present bivouacs.

3. Field Companies R.E. and Pioneers will move at dusk on "Y" day to the forward bivouacs selected East of VIERSTRAAT- YPRES road, movement to be completed by 10.0.p.m. on "Y" day. Wagon lines remaining in present position.

4. 237th Field Coy. R.E. will construct a pontoon bridge at O.4.a.7.7. at dusk on "Y" day in accordance with instructions issued previously dated July 23rd.

5. Reference 41st Division Instruction No.2. issued with 41st Div. G.784 the detail of work for "Z" day and "Z/A" night is recapitulated and amplified as follows.

6. 1 Section 1st Canadian Tunnelling Coy. R.E. will reconnoitre and search for deep dugouts and mine charges in or about HOLLEBEKE village and in the railway embankment in O.6.a. and repair for occupation any deep dugouts found.

7. 228th Field Coy. R.E. with attached infantry less 1 section and 1 platoon detached under orders of the 122nd Infantry Brigade will carry out the consolidation of the RED LINE in front of the line of OBLIQUE TRENCH and connecting to the line of OPTIC TRENCH. This line will be laid out by Major W.L. SHAW R.E. and will be continuously wired.
    A footbridge will be constructed across the canal approximately on the line of OBLIQUE TRENCH to connect the RED LINE across the canal. Further sites forward should be reconnoitred and preparations made for footbridges at three additional sites, material being collected at points selected.
    A tracing party under an officer will lay out for the 122nd Infantry Brigade working party a line for a Communication Trench to carry forward OAR AVENUE - OBLIQUE ROW to the GREEN LINE.
    A signboarding patrol will signboard the RED LINE and all trenches leading up to it.

8. 233rd Field Coy. R.E. with attached infantry less 1 section and 1 platoon detailed with 123rd Infantry Brigade will carry out the consolidation of the RED LINE on the line of strong posts RAILWAY EMBANKMENT O.6.a.4.4½. corner of wood O.6.a.9.7., I.36.d.2.0., I.30.d.5.5. This line will be laid out by Major H.P.O. THWAITES R.E. and will be continuously wired.
    A tracing party under an officer will lay out for the 123rd Infantry Brigade working party a line for a Communication Trench to carry forward IMTACT TERRACE-IMPARTIAL AVENUE to the GREEN LINE.
    A signboarding patrol will signboard the RED LINE and all trenches leading up to it.

2.

9. The 237th Field Coy. R.E. with attached infantry will maintain the pontoon bridge across the canal at O.4.a.7.7. and its approaches, also the bridge at NORFOLK LOCK and its approaches, keeping the approach to NORFOLK BRIDGE from I.33.c.4.2. open for the use of motor ambulances and maintaining and extending the canal road as a transport track to BUFFS BANK. Footbridges and approaches from this track to be made at approximately the position of the old German bridges O.5.a.5.2., O.5.a.7.3., and O.5.b.1.4.

   A signboarding patrol will signboard the crossings of the canal, transport routes and overland tracks.

10. 19th Bn. Middlesex Regt. (Pioneers)

"A" Coy. Continue OAK AVENUE on the alignment OAK LANE-OAK ROW-OAK KEEP to the BLUE LINE at about O.6.b.4.4. and forward to the GREEN LINE.

"B" Coy. Continue OPTIC AVENUE from present front line to the BLUE LINE at about O.11.b.7.3. and forward to the GREEN LINE, and will also maintain OPTIC ROAD and transport track from ST ELOI to OPTIC AVENUE and pack route parallel to OPTIC AVENUE to the HOLLEBEKE road.

"C" Coy. Maintain tram line system from SHELLEY DUMP and from BRICKSTACK to R.A.P's Nos. 3 & 4. Maintain tram line along South bank of canal from NORFOLK BRIDGE and crossing to siding below IMP DUMP and high level line from above IMP DUMP to R.A.P's Nos. 1 & 2. Extend low level line along North bank of canal from IMP DUMP to BUFFS BANK.

"D" Coy. Maintain and improve transport routes:-
 (a) CATERPILLAR TRACK from the Corps road North of LA CHAPELLE FARM at I.27.d.7.3. to RAVINE WOOD I.34.a.6.3. along the line of IMPERIAL TRENCH from I.34.d.3.9. to the North end of the CATERPILLAR and pack route thence along the East side of the CATERPILLAR towards KLEIN ZILLEBEKE.
 (b) From NORFOLK BRIDGE (I.33.d.2.5.) to RAVINE WOOD (I.34.a.6.4.)
 (c) From the BLUFF CRATERS (O.4.a.7.9.) along the line of IMPUDENCE TRENCH to I.31.d.3.9.

11. The consolidation parties of 228th and 233rd Field Coys. R.E. will move forward under orders of the Divisional Commander conveyed through C.R.E.. All other parties will proceed to work as soon after the zero hour as the situation admits.

12. Telegraphic reports will be rendered during operations by each unit to reach C.R.E. at Divisional Hd. Qrs. by 8.0.a.m. daily on work of previous night, and written reports giving detail of work of the previous 24 hours with hand sketches showing position and character of work done to reach C.R.E. by 4.30.p.m. daily.

13. Zero hour will be notified later.

14.  ACKNOWLEDGE.

         *M Wockley*

         Lieut. Colonel R.E.
         C.R.E. 41st Division.

# WAR DIARY or INTELLIGENCE SUMMARY

Army Form C. 2118

ORIGINAL

H.Q. 41st Div'n ENGINEERS  Vol 16

AUGUST 1917

| Place | Date | Hour | Summary of Events and Information | Remarks and references to Appendices |
|---|---|---|---|---|
| WESTOUTRE | 1 | | B.M. went despatched to the 228th and 237th Field Coys and the 19th Middlesex Pioneers, expressing the Divn Commanders pleasure with the previous days reports of work carried out by them. 228th Fd. Co. engaged on footbridge over Canal, consolidating Red Line & reclaiming old German communication trench. 237th Fd. Co. reported that road on N. side of Canal between NORFOLK and Pontoon bridges and the approach to the bridge on the S. side of Canal were all open for traffic. 19th Middlesex Pioneers engaged in clearing & containing OPTIC TRENCH. Owing to heavy rain all work was reported very difficult. | |
| | 3 | | 228th Fd. Co. New C.T from O.S.c.8.6 to O.S.d.3.6. 233rd " " Consolidation of RED LINE. 237th " " Widening & improving approaches to NORFOLK BRIDGE, and the construction of a heavy bridge over DIEPENDAALBEEK at O.8.c.80.95. | |
| | 4 | | Captain N.D.R. HUNTER relinquished acting ranks of Captain & Adjutant & since proceeding on the 29-7-17 for duty with the 233rd Fd. Co. adjutants duty was undertaken by 2nd Lieut H.A. DICKMAN | |

**Army Form C. 2118**

# WAR DIARY
or
## INTELLIGENCE SUMMARY
*(Erase heading not required.)*

**AUGUST 1917**     **H.Q. 41st Divnl. ENGINEERS**

| Place | Date | Hour | Summary of Events and Information | Remarks and references to Appendices |
|---|---|---|---|---|
| WESTOUTRE | 4 | | 237th Fd. Co. Artillery bridge at O.8.c.80.95 not being considered suitable as a permanent structure was potentials removed and replaced. | |
| | | | 233rd Fd. Co. Commenced work on IMPACT - IMPARTIAL AVENUE | |
| | | | 19th Middlesex Regt. (Pioneers) New C.T. between O.A.b.5.8 - O.S.a.4.5 & laying duckboard track to O.S.a.3.8. Completing tramway nr NORFOLK BRIDGE | |
| | 5 | | Lieut. A.S. GLOVER, 233rd Field Co. commenced duties of acting adjutant. 2/Lieut. H.A. DICKMAN " " returned to Company for duty. | |
| | | | 19th Middlesex Regt. (Pioneers) Duckboard track OAF AVENUE to FRONT LINE | |
| | | | 228th Field Co. Double duckboard track thro' WHITE CHATEAU WOOD. | |
| | 6 | | 237th Field Co. Artillery bridge at O.8.C.80.95 completed and made suitable for all traffic. Provided parties to salvage R.E material from old front & support lines & disused C.T.s and store in forward R.E dumps. | |
| | | | 233rd Field Co. Continuing duckboard track through BATTLE WOOD to front line | |
| | | | 228th Field Co. Connecting up RED LINE to O.C.C.T through wood at O.S.d.73.57 | |

# WAR DIARY
## or
## INTELLIGENCE SUMMARY

Army Form C. 2118

AUGUST 1917          H.Q. 41st DIVNL ENGINEERS.

| Place | Date | Hour | Summary of Events and Information | Remarks and references to Appendices |
|---|---|---|---|---|
| WESTOUTRE | 7 | | 19th Middlesex Batt. (Pioneers) Commenced duckboard track alongside tram from DAMMSTRASSE to FRONT LINE owing to OPTIC AVENUE being impassable owing to floods. | |
| | | | 233rd Field Co. R.E. Proceeded with continuation of TRAMWALK through BATTLE WOOD with single duckboard track. | |
| | | | 237th Field Co. Reported that "A" and "D" tunnels to CANAL SUBWAY had been cleared and made fit for use. | |
| | 8 | | 2nd Lieut. J.W. SMITH. 237th Field Co. commenced duties as assistant adjutant. | |
| | | | 237th Field Co. Commenced work connecting "A" and "D" tunnels to CANAL SUBWAY by trenches to CANAL ROAD. | |
| | | | 228th Field Co Completed double duck board track from tramway line to E. edge of WHITE CHATEAU WOOD. Wiring new front line from O.11.d.2.9 to O.1.6.5.1 (FORRET FARM) | |
| | | | 233rd Field Co. Wiring on left of front line posts. | |
| | | | 19th Middlesex Regt. (Pioneers) Duckboard work thro' OAF AVENUE to SPOIL BANK reported completed. RAILWAY EMBANKMENT Completed. Track from NORFOLK BRIDGE over SPOIL BANK reported completed. | |

Army Form C. 2118

# WAR DIARY
## or
## INTELLIGENCE SUMMARY
(Erase heading not required.)

AUGUST 1917　　　H.Q. 41st Div^n Engineers

| Place | Date | Hour | Summary of Events and Information | Remarks and references to Appendices |
|---|---|---|---|---|
| WESTOUTRE | 9. | | 237th Field Co. 2/Lieut J.R. STRATTON wounded in action. Owing to heavy intermittent shell fire over the area of the works in progress, together with the recent heavy rain, work generally has been very much curtailed for this and preceding days. 237th Field Co. reported that the entrance to CANAL SUBWAY from CANAL ROAD were completed. 2nd Lieut. W.L. HAMILTON reported for duty and was posted to this company. | |
| | 10 | | 237th Field Co. reported that the stretcher tracks from NORFOLK LOCK gate to NORFOLK LOCK BRIDGE had been made passable for carrying and wheeling stretchers. 19th Middlesex Regt. (Pioneers) reported that the OAF AVENUE trench and duckboard track to Railway Embankment was completed as far as the RAVINE. | |
| | 12 | | Lt. H.M. BOYD. 233rd Field Co. proceeded to ENGLAND to take up duty at CHATHAM. | |

# WAR DIARY or INTELLIGENCE SUMMARY

**Army Form C. 2118**

AUGUST 1917    H.Q. 41ST DIVN ENGINEERS

| Place | Date | Hour | Summary of Events and Information | Remarks and references to Appendices |
|---|---|---|---|---|
| WESTOUTRE | 13 | | 228th Field Co. moved from BOIS CARRE to rest billets in the BERTHEN area. | |
| | 14 | | 233rd " " " " " " " " " " " | |
| | " | | 237th " " " " " " " " " " " | |
| | 15 | | H.Q 41st Division relieved by 39th Division at WESTOUTRE and moved to BERTHEN area. | |
| | | | H.Q. R.E. moved its billets at R.21.a.2.8 | |
| BERTHEN | 16 | | 2nd LIEUT. S.C. BONNIWELL. R.E. reported for duty and proceeded to the 237th Field Co. | |
| " | 17 | 9.0am | The Divisional Commander inspected the divisional R.E.s and attached Infantry at R.21.a.2.8 and afterwards thanked the C.R.E., Field Co. Commanders, Officers and other ranks for the very satisfactory work carried out in preparation for and since the offensive of the 31st JULY last. | |
| " | 18 | | 2nd LIEUT. J. GRAY. R.E proceeded to XIth Corps School C.R.E. and Adjutant attended the 2nd Army Commander's inspection of 122nd, 123rd, 124th Inf. Brigades | |

Army Form C. 2118

# WAR DIARY
## or
## INTELLIGENCE SUMMARY
*(Erase heading not required.)*

H.Q. 41st DIV: ENGINEERS

AUGUST 1917

| Place | Date | Hour | Summary of Events and Information | Remarks and references to Appendices |
|---|---|---|---|---|
| BERTHEN | 21 | | H.Q. R.E. moved into rest billets at WIZERNES along with Divisional H.Q. | |
| WIZERNES | 24 | 11 A.M | C.R.E and Adjutant attended the inspection of the Division – less the 124th Inf. Brigade Group – by the C in C at LE FOSSE Farm W.23.a.6.4 | |
| | | | 124th Infy Bde Group – less 237th Field Co. R.E. moved from THIEUSHOUK area into TATINGHEM | |
| | 25 | | " " " " | |
| | 26 | | 237th Field Co. moved from THIEUSHOUK to MILLEKRUISSE | |
| | 27 | | " " employed under the direction of C.E. Xth Corps from this date | |
| | 29 | 10 A.M | C.R.E attended a conference at C.E's office Xth Corps H.Q. on Trench Tramways. | |
| | 30 | | 233rd and 228th Field Co. and 19th Middlesex Regt (Pioneers) moved forward into 39th Divn area and were accommodated as follows. | |
| | | | 233rd and 228th Field Cos at N.S. 6.0.8 and 19th Middlesex Regt (Pioneers) at N.8.6.1.3 and H.35.d.6.2. | |

Army Form C. 2118

# WAR DIARY
## or
## INTELLIGENCE SUMMARY

(Erase heading not required.)

H.Q. 41st. Divl. ENGINEERS

AUG — 1917

| Place | Date | Hour | Summary of Events and Information | Remarks and references to Appendices |
|---|---|---|---|---|
| WIZERNES | 31 | | 233rd and 228th Field Coy. and 19th. Middlesex Regt. (Pioneers) employed under the control of C.E. XIth Corps from this date. | |
| | | 6-9-17 | | |

SMMorrey Lieut Col
CRE 41st Div.

## 41st DIVISIONAL ENGINEERS.

Return of HONOURS & REWARDS and CASUALTIES from 21.10.1916 to 21.6.1917.

### ST ELOI AREA.

|  |  | Off. | O.R. |
|---|---|---|---|
| HONOURS AND REWARDS. | 228th Field Coy | 3 | 2 |
|  | 233rd    "      " | 2 | 4 |
|  | 237th    "      " | 2 | 2 |
|  | H.Q., R.E. 41 Div. | 1 | - |
|  | Total. | 8 | 8 |
| KILLED IN ACTION. | 228th Field Coy. | - | 3 |
|  | 233rd    "      " | - | 1 |
|  | 237th    "      " | 1 | 2 |
|  | Total. | 1 | 6 |
| DIED OF WOUNDS. | 228th Field Coy. | 1 | 1 |
|  | 233rd    "      " | 1 | 6 |
|  | 237th    "      " | - | 1 |
|  | Total. | 2 | 8 |
| WOUNDED AND EVACUATED. | 228th Field Coy. | 2 | 22 |
|  | 233rd    "      " | - | 18 |
|  | 237th    "      " | 1 | 28 |
|  | Total. | 3 | 68 |
| WOUNDED & RETURNED to DUTY. | 228th Field Coy. | - | 8 |
|  | 233rd    "      " | - | 6 |
|  | 237th    "      " | - | 5 |
|  | Total. | - | 19 |
| EVACUATED SICK | 228th Field Coy. | - | 38 |
|  | 233rd    "      " | - | 22 |
|  | 237th    "      " | 1 | 16 |
|  | Total. | 1 | 76 |

|  |  | Off. | O.R. |
|---|---|---|---|
| Total | HONOURS & REWARDS. | 8 | 8 |
|  | CASUALTIES | 6 | 168. |

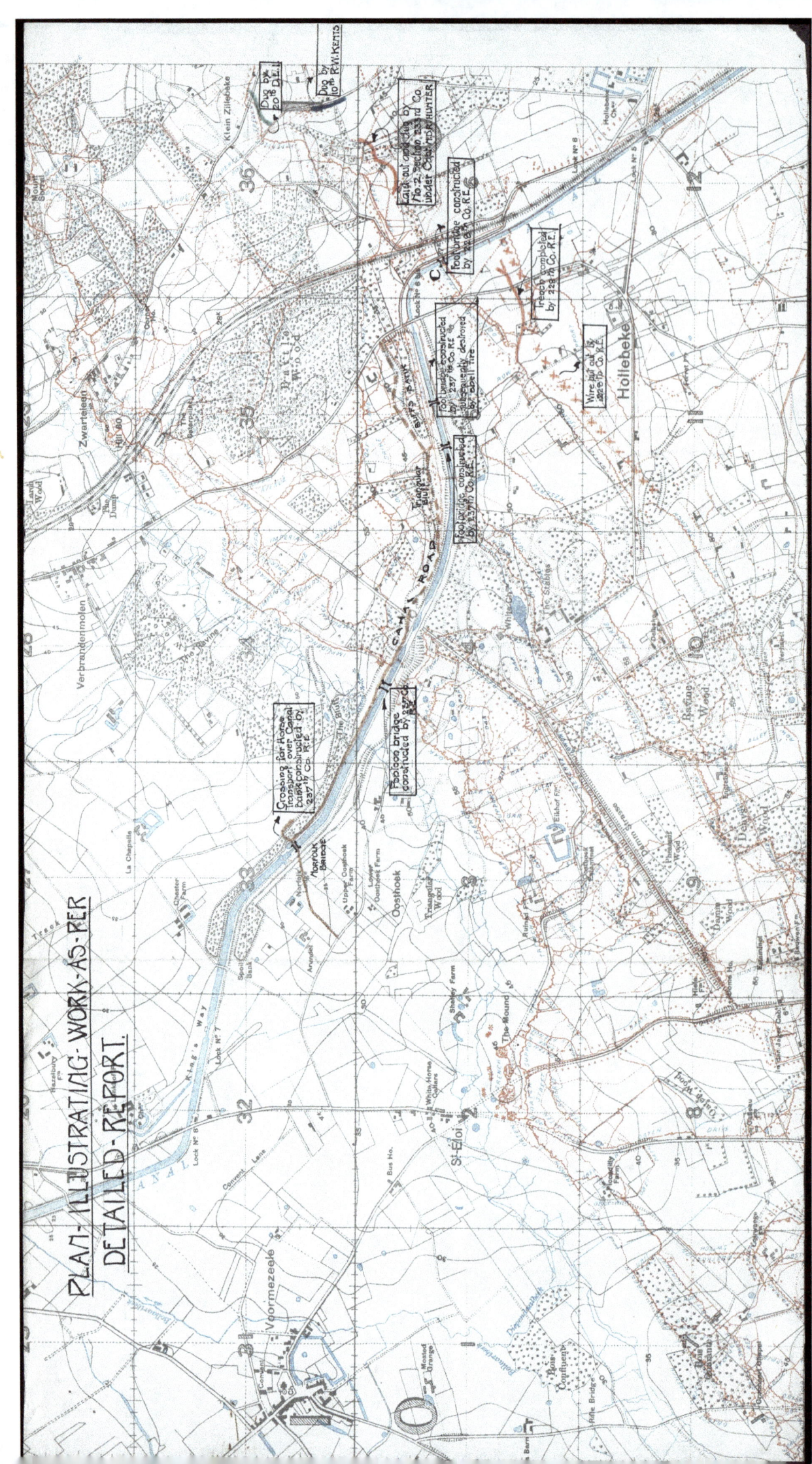

ORIGINAL

Army Form C. 2118

# WAR DIARY
## or
## INTELLIGENCE SUMMARY
*(Erase heading not required.)*

SEPT. 1917        H.Q. 41st DIV. ENGINEERS

Vol 17

| Place | Date | Hour | Summary of Events and Information | Remarks and references to Appendices |
|---|---|---|---|---|
| WIZERNES | 3 | | H.Q. moved with advanced DIV. H.Q. to LA CLYTE and were temporarily accommodated in the vacated C.C.S at N.7.C.3.4½. | |
| LA CLYTE | 5 | | The Divisional R.E.s and Pioneers (with the exception of "C" and "D" Companies) ceased to be employed under the direction of the C.E. XII Corps. | |
| " | 6 | | The R.E.s and Pioneers of the 41st Div commenced to be employed in the BODMIN COPSE – LOWER STAR POST sector of the line, and were detailed for work as under. | |
| | | | 228th Field Co. work in the left (Brigade) sector in MT SORREL, hastening out to the assembly trench work from HEDGE STREET to GREEN JACKET RIDE overland tracks from BODMIN COPSE at about J.19.d.2.6. J.19.C.0.0 and bifurcation to BODMIN COPSE at about J.19.d.4.1 and to J.19.d.4.1. | |
| | | | 233rd Field Co. work in Reserve Brigade sector, including the improvement of R.A.P in CANADA STREET to accommodate 40 stretchers and C.P in LARCH WOOD to provide for a like number of stretchers. | |
| | | | 237th Field Co. work in Right Brigade sector, including a duckboard track for Right Brigade within the Boundary Dis' Boundary MT SORREL to LOWER STAR POST, with bifurcation from about J.25.a.3.2 to about J.25.b.2½.6½. | |

1875  Wt. W593/826  1,000,000  4/15  J.B.C. & A.  A.D.S.S./Forms/C. 2118.

Army Form C. 2118

# WAR DIARY or INTELLIGENCE SUMMARY

(Erase heading not required.)

H.Q. 41ST. DIV: ENGINEERS

SEPT. 1917

| Place | Date | Hour | Summary of Events and Information | Remarks and references to Appendices |
|---|---|---|---|---|
| LA CLYTE | 11 | | 19th Middlesex (Pioneers) were detailed for work as under. Complete assembly of engineer work already in hand in MT. SORREL after which assist with work detailed for "B" Coy. | |
| | | | "A" Coy. | |
| | | | "B" Coy. Duckboard walk from Left Brigade southern Boundary from KNOLL ROAD at about I.29.a.4.5.82. Divisional Boundary from KNOLL ROAD to HEDGE STREET. | |
| | | | "C" Coy. Tramline from CANADA STREET RAP to LARCHWOOD A.D.S. | |
| | | | "D" Coy. Construction of Pack route from junction of plank road and railway at I.28.b.4.8 to KNOLL FARM and thence to CANADA STREET and HEDGE STREET. | |
| " | 12 | | Major E. MOORE M.C. R.E. assumed command of the 233rd. Field Co. | |
| " | 14 | | LT. G.A. HARRIS of the 233rd. Field Co. assumed command of the 42nd. A.T. Coy. | |
| " | 15 | | H.Q. 41st Divn. moved from WIZERNES, together with advanced Divl. H.Q. from LA CLYTE, and took over from the 24th Divn. at ZEVECOTEN G.35.d.1.0 | |
| ZEVECOTEN | 17-18 | | 41st Divn. relieved the 23rd. and 39th. Divisions in the line. | |
| " | 20 | 5.40AM | The 41st Divn. attacked on a front between LOWER STAR POST to JAVA AVENUE | |

Army Form C. 2118

# WAR DIARY
## or
## INTELLIGENCE SUMMARY
(Erase heading not required.)

H.Q. 41ST DIVN ENGINEERS

SEPT 1917.

| Place | Date | Hour | Summary of Events and Information | Remarks and references to Appendices |
|---|---|---|---|---|
| ZEVECOTEN | 21 | | Col. T. E. N. STOCKLEY departed for ENGLAND on Sick Leave. MAJOR. C. L. T. MATHESON. O.C. 237th Field Co. took over as acting C.R.E. | |
| CAESTRE | 23 | | 41st Div. H.Q. moved from ZEVECOTEN to CAESTRE. | |
| " | 22/23 | | The 39th Div. took over the whole of the 41st Div. front in the line. The Div. R.E. and Pioneers were employed under the 39th Divn. from the 23rd. | |
| " | 24 | | | |
| " | 25 | | Field Coys and Pioneers left RIDGEWOOD AREA and proceeded to CAESTRE AREA. | |
| " | 26 | | H.Q. R.E. left CAESTRE and proceeded to LA PANNE. (During XV Corps, 4th Army Area.) Major C. L. T. MATHESON. R.E. left to proceed to ENGLAND to take up duties as Sr. Instructor in Field Engineering at R.M.A. WOOLWICH. | |
| LA PANNE | 26 | | Major E. MOORE. R.E. joined H.Q. R.E. as acting C.R.E. | |

5-10-17

E. Moore Lieut Colonel
C.R.E. 41st Divn

## 41st Divisional Engineers.

### Return of Honours and Rewards and Casualties from 16th Aug.1917 to Sept. 30th,1917.

|  |  | Off. | O.R. |
|---|---|---|---|
| Honours and Rewards. | 228th Field Coy. | 2 | 1. |
|  | 233rd  "    " | 1. | 3. |
|  | 237th  "    " | - | 3. |
|  |  | 3. | 7. |
| Killed in action. | 228th Field Coy. | 1. | 1. |
|  | 233rd  "    " | - | - |
|  | 237th  "    " | 1. | 4. |
|  |  | 2. | 5. |
| Died of Wounds. |  | NIL. | |
| Wounded and Evacuated. | 228th Field Coy. | 1. | 12. |
|  | 233rd  "    " | - | 8. |
|  | 237th  "    " | - | 3. |
|  |  | 1. | 23. |
| Wounded slightly at Duty. | 228th Field Coy. | - | 7 |
|  | 233rd  "    " | - | - |
|  | 237th  "    " | - | 1 |
|  |  | - | 8. |
| Missing. | 228th Field Coy. | - | 2 |
|  | 233rd  "    " | - | - |
|  | 237th  "    " | - | 1. |
|  |  | - | 3. |
| Evacuated sick. | 228th Field Coy. | - | 12. |
|  | 233rd  "    " | - | 11. |
|  | 237th  "    " | - | 13. |
|  |  | - | 36. |

### Total since May 1st 1916.

|  | Off. | O.R. |
|---|---|---|
| Honours and awards. | 14. | 29. |
| Casualties. | 16. | 337. (337) |

## Casualties.  Attched Infantry.

|  |  | Off. | O.R. |
|---|---|---|---|
| Killed in action | 228th Field Coy. | - | 2. |
|  | 233rd    "      " | - | - |
|  | 237th    "      " | - | - |
|  |  | - | 2 |
| Wounded and Evac. | 228th   "      " | - | 21. |
|  | 233rd   "      " | - | 4. |
|  | 237th   "      " | - | 4. |
|  |  | - | 29. |
| Wounded at Duty. | 228th   "      " | - | 3 |
|  | 233rd   "      " | - | 1. |
|  | 237th   "      " | - | - |
|  |  | - | 4 |
| Missing. | 228th   "      " | - | - |
|  | 233rd   "      " | - | - |
|  | 237th   "      " | - | 1. |
|  |  | - | 1. |
| Evacuated sick. | 228th   "      " | 1. | 13. |
|  | 233rd   "      " | - | 9 |
|  | 237th   "      " | - | 7. |
|  |  | 1. | 29. |

S E C R E T.

C O P Y  N O. 8

### C.R.E'S OPERATION ORDER NO. T.H. 2.

18th September, 1917.

1. The 41st Division will attack on "E" day in accordance with orders and instructions already issued. Zero hour will be notified later.

2. Field Coys. and Pioneers will rest on "D" day in their present bivouacs.

3. The detail of work for attack day will be as in table attached to 41st Division Instruction No.10 dated 13.9.1917.

4. Working parties will move forward to carry out this work commencing work as under:-

| | | |
|---|---|---|
| 228th Field Coy. (Less 1 section & 1 platoon) | For consolidation of BLUE LINE. | O.C. Coy. to confer with G.O.C. Bde as to situation on GREEN LINE. Working parties to arrive at HEDGE STREET and CANADA STREET 5 hours after Zero and advance to work as soon as situation in GREEN LINE is clear. |
| 237th Field Coy. (Less 1 section & 1 platoon) | do. | |
| "A" Coy.) 19th Bn. "B" Coy.) Middsex Regt. | For routes "B" and "D" | (2 hours after Zero if (situation admits. |
| "C" Coy. 19th Bn. Middsex Regt. | Tramline forward extension. | (3 hours after Zero if (situation admits. |
| "D" Coy. 19th Bn. Middsex Regt. | Pack route. Forward extension. | (3 hours after Zero if (situation admits. |

5. Telegraphic reports will be rendered during operations by each unit to reach C.R.E. at D.H.Q. by 8.0.a.m. daily on work of previous night, and written reports giving detail of work of previous 24 hours, numbers employed and hand sketches showing character and position of work to reach C.R.E. by 5.0.p.m. daily.

6. Telephonic communication is established with the 228th Field Coy. R.E. at RIDGE WOOD, N.5.b.0.8, and orderlies from each other Field Coy. and 19th Bn. Middlesex Regt. will be posted there to take messages for their units.

7. ACKNOWLEDGE.

Lieut. Colonel R.E.

C.R.E. 41st Division.

```
Copy No.1      228th Field Coy. R.E.
Copy No.2      233rd Field Coy. R.E.
 "    " 3.    237th Field Coy. R.E.
 "    " 4.    19th Bn. Middlesex Regt.
 "    " 5.    41st Division "G".
 "    " 6.    41st Division "Q".
 "    " 7.    122nd Infantry Brigade.
 "    " 8.    123rd Infantry Brigade.
 "    " 9.    124th Infantry Brigade.
 "    "10.    C.R.E. 23rd Division.
 "    "11.    C.R.E. 39th Division.
 "    "12.    C.E. Xth Corps.
 "    "13.    C.R.E. 41st Division.
```

} for information

ORIGINAL

Army Form C. 2118

# WAR DIARY
## or
## INTELLIGENCE SUMMARY

(Erase heading not required.)

H.Qrs. R.E. 41st Division    Vol 18

Oct 1917

| Place | Date | Hour | Summary of Events and Information | Remarks and references to Appendices |
|---|---|---|---|---|
| LA PANNE | Oct.1st | | Major E. Moore, M.E. R.E., acting CRE and Capt. A.S. Glover R.E., Adjutant, visited CREs of 32nd and 42nd Division to obtain information concerning work in hand in their respective Divisional Fronts. It was not decided at this date which of these Divisions the 41st Division would relieve. | |
| " | 3rd | | Lt.Col. F.W. Stockley DSO R.E. Returned to duty from England. | |
| " | 4th | | CRE, Col. Parker, G.S.O.1, and CRE of 42nd Division went with Branches on 42nd Divl Front with a view to taking over. | |
| " | 5th | | CRE & Adjutant visited Corps R.E. Park at DUNKERKE | |
| " | 6th | | CRE visited billets and horse lines of Field Companies | |
| " | 7th | | Divisional Headquarters moved to ST. IDESBALD and relieved the 42nd Dn. H.Q.R.E. took over billets | |
| ST. IDESBALD | 8th | | CRE + Col. Riddell D.S.O., A.A & Q.M.G., selected sites for camps, huts and stables in Divisional Area. | |
| " | 9th | | CRE, Adjutant & Medical Officer visited billets of 233rd Field Coy. R.E. in the village of NIEUPORT BAINS | |
| " | 10th | | C.E. XV Corps, Brig. Gen. Sergent, called at this office and informed the CRE that arrangements were to be made to collect stores, BERTHON boats, pontoon equipment &c. & prepare for bridging the R. YSER sites for the training of the Field Coys. in this work were chosen on the DUNKERKE - FURNES Canal. | |

Army Form C. 2118

# WAR DIARY
## or
## INTELLIGENCE SUMMARY
(Erase heading not required.)

H.Qrs. R.E. 66th Division

Oct. 1917

| Place | Date | Hour | Summary of Events and Information | Remarks and references to Appendices |
|---|---|---|---|---|
| ST. IDESBALD | 11th | | Bridging stores were assembled and a "Bridging Yard" formed at Manchester Dump. The Divisional R.E. Dump near COXYDE. The 225th Fld Coy R.E. were made responsible for thin Bridge boats and the 237th Fld Coy R.E. were detailed for practice at Pontooning & Constructing Barrel Pier Bridges. Major Reid R.E. O.C. 237th Fld Coy, and Adjutant visited the C.R.E. H.Qrs. at BRAY DUNES to arrange for a camp for 237th Field Coy near GHYVELDE in order that they might be near the Pontooning "Grand". | |
| " " | 12th | | The C.R.E. went round front line Trenches with Major E. Moore O.C. 233rd Field Coy R.E. | |
| " " | 13th | | Major Eric Buckland, C.S. II Army called at C.R.E. & discussed Bridging Operations. Major Garforth R.E., Major Gracie R.E., Major Reid O.C. Field Coy commanders & C.B. "Dis" arrived and went into details of Bridging Operations into C.H.Q. Major Shaw & Major Reid — My scheme of the 66th Division preparing Sheetfor Division occupied thin Section, was adopted as a basis for training. | |
| " " | 14th | | Major Garforth R.E., Major Reid O.C. 237th Fld Coy R.E. visited site chosen for Pontoon Bays & Pier Bridges. Major Gracie and Major Shaw O.C. 225th Field Coy visited the proposed sites for rafts with Barker Boats. | |

1875 Wt. W593/826 1,000,000 4/15 J.B.C. & A. A.D.S.S./Forms/C. 2118.

# WAR DIARY or INTELLIGENCE SUMMARY

Army Form C. 2118

H.Qrs. R.E. 41st Division

Oct. 1917

| Place | Date | Hour | Summary of Events and Information | Remarks and references to Appendices |
|---|---|---|---|---|
| ST. DESBALD | 15th | | The CRE visited Bridging Training on the DUNKERKE-FURNES CANAL with Brig. Gen. Serrick, acting Divisional Commander, and Maj. Gen. Backland, C.G. II Army. | |
| " | 16th | | The CRE and Adjutant visited Bridging Training at St. Elsye, and then proceeded to DUNKERKE to purchase stores for Bazaar Opt.Repairs. They then visited FORT PHILIPPE and examined the Estuary of the River AA with a view to finding a suitable field river for Bridging Training of the Field Companies. This Estuary was not considered suitable.  During the night 16th–17th ST DESBALD was shelled by H.V. Guns. H.Q. R.E. billets received two direct hits which wrecked the C.R.E's Mess & the Officers Kitchen. There were fortunately no Casualties. The writer was asleep in a dug out near by. | |
| " | 17th | | The CRE, GOC, Maj. Gen. Sibele, U.S. Army, his chief of Staff, Col. Williams two A.D.C. from the Divisional R.E. Dump-Workshops and also visited the Field Coys at Bray-Dunes Practice, Bolani  to them the General Scheme of Manoeuvres for them. They also inspected the Transport Horses of 228th Field Coy & R.E. The Adjutant arranged for high billets with Are Commandant ST DESBALD and H.Q R.E. moved into them during the afternoon. | |

# WAR DIARY or INTELLIGENCE SUMMARY

Army Form C. 2118

H.Qrs. R.E. 41st Division

Oct 1917

| Place | Date | Hour | Summary of Events and Information | Remarks and references to Appendices |
|---|---|---|---|---|
| ST. IDESBALD | 19 | | The CRE visited the Bridging Training of Field Coys in the morning. In the afternoon he visited CR XV Corps at BRAY DUNES | |
| | 20 | | The CRE visited huts & stables in the LA PANNE - ST IDESBALD area. The Adjutant attended conference at C.E. XV Corps Office to discuss arrangements for operation with C.E.R.O. for the handing of R.E. Stores by Dist & Railways in the Corps Area. | |
| | 21 | | Orders were received that one Field Coy. and one coy. of Pioneers (19th Middlesex) were to be handed over to work under the C.R.E. 42nd Division in his Divisional Sector. The Coys sent of 225th Field Coy at LA PANNE. The CRE visited Major Stand D.C. The CRE visited details of the CRE Adjutant visited the Bridging Train the Div. Commander, G.S.O.I. taken across the Canal by means of rafts and saw 2 battalions [crossing]. Broken boats. | |
| | 22 | | 2nd Lieut J.W. Smyth left to take up duties under CRE ABBEVILLE. Lieut E.P. Adam RE 228th Field Coy. was attached H.Q. R.E. as Acting Officer. | |

# WAR DIARY
## or
## INTELLIGENCE SUMMARY

Army Form C. 2118

Headquarters R.E. 41st Division

Oct. 1917

| Place | Date | Hour | Summary of Events and Information | Remarks and references to Appendices |
|---|---|---|---|---|
| ST. IDESBALD | 24th | | The CRE & Adjutant went round trenches with G.S.O.1 and saw the work being done by 233rd Field Coy R.E. They were also shown round the various works by Major Moore, O.C. 233rd Field Coy R.E. | |
| " " | 25th | | The CRE visited the Bridging Training Camp & put up by 237th Field Coy R.E. the 228th Field Coy now working under CRE 42nd Division. | |
| " " | 27th | | CRE and Adjutant visited 237th Field Coy at BRAY DUNES and also inspected pontoon and bomb firing equipment prior to its being handed over to 233rd Field Coy R.E. | |
| " " | 28th | | Orders were received at 4 a.m. to the effect that 41st Division would be relieved by 9th Division on 29th; CRE 9th Division called and discussed R.E. work in hand with a view to taking over. Rafts between 237th & 233rd Field Coys cancelled. 237th Field Coy moved to TETEGHEM AREA. | |
| " " | 29th | | 9th Division relieved 41st Div CRE handed over all plans, maps & bridging scheme to CRE 9th Division. Adjutant showed | |

# WAR DIARY or INTELLIGENCE SUMMARY

Army Form C. 2118

Headquarters R.E. 41st Division

Month: Oct. 1917

| Place | Date | Hour | Summary of Events and Information | Remarks and references to Appendices |
|---|---|---|---|---|
| ST. IDESBALD | 29 | | Adjutant R.E. g/h Div. found Divisional R.E. Dump and Workshops. These were then taken over by 9th Division H.Qrs. 41st Division moved to MALO-LES-BAINS. C.R.E's Office at 89 Avenue Belaire. 226th Field Coy R.E. moved to PETIT SYNTHE AREA. | |
| MALO-LES-BAINS | 30 | | 233rd Field Coy R.E. relieved by 90th Field Coy R.E. and proceeded to BRAY DUNES. | |
| " " | 31 | | C.R.E. visited 233rd Field Coy at BRAY DUNES and arranged for them to carry on Pontoon practice during such time as they remained at BRAY DUNES. C.E. XV Corps gave permission for use of Pontoons of 12th Pontoon Park. | |

J. Moseley
Lt.Col. R.E.
C.R.E. 41st Division

1-11-17

S E C R E T.    COPY NO...7...

C.R.E'S OPERATION ORDER C.S. No.1.

4th October, 1917.

Reference 41st Div. Order No.177 para. 9. relief of the R.E. and Pioneers will be arranged for as under. All works, billets and wagon lines to be taken over from corresponding unit.

(a) NIEUPORT BAINS SECTOR.

233rd Field Coy. R.E. will relieve the 429th Field Coy. R.E. on the 6th instant. Relief to be completed by 6.0.p.m.

(b) COXIDE BAINS COAST DEFENCE SECTOR.

237th Field Coy. R.E. will relieve the 428th Field Coy. R.E. on the 6th instant. Relief to be completed by 6.0.p.m.

(c) RESERVE SECTOR.

228th Field Coy. R.E. will relieve the 427th Field Coy. R.E. on the 5th instant. Relief to be completed by 6.0.p.m.

(d) PIONEER BATTALION.

19th Bn. Middlesex Regt. will relieve the 6th Bn. Welch Regt. on the 7th instant. Relief to be completed by midday.

2. A Divisional Programme of Work will be issued shortly; in the meantime the allotment of work is as follows:-

(1) 233rd Field Coy. R.E. work on the Front, Support and Reserve Lines including all work taken over from the 429th Field Coy.

(2) 237th Field Coy. work on artillery positions, wiring of AEOLIAN ROAD, XVth Corps M.G. position and other work other than communications and trench tramways which the 428th Field Coy. has in hand.

(3) 228th Field Coy. work on Hutments, stabling and accommodation in Reserve area; and completion of Advanced Divisional Hd. Qrs.

(4) 19th Bn. Middlesex Regt.
"A" Coy. BATH AVENUE EXTENSION, BATH and BLIGHTY AVENUES, BATH LANE, BEACH AVENUE and BRIDGE STREET.
"B" Coy. BOCHE EXTENSION, BOCHE AVENUE, BOCHE LANE.
"C" Coy. Tramline programme as in hand.
"D" Coy. Road maintenance and programme as in hand.

2.

Arrangements for R.E. stores will be as follows:-

Divisional R.E. Dump is MANCHESTER DUMP on road between COXYDE and OOST DUNKERKE at X.8.d.3.8.

Field Companies R.E. and Pioneers may draw from this dump on their own indent.

Field Coy. Dumps will be:- for 233rd Field Coy. No.1 Advanced dump at R.23.d.4.4. (Laitorie) - for 237th Field Coy. at No. 2 Advanced Dump at M.25.c.1.9..

Field Companies will stock these dumps from MANCHESTER DUMP for the present.

*Stockley*
Lieut. Colonel R.E.
C.R.E. 41st Division.

```
Copy No.  1.  228th Field Coy. R.E.
 "   "    2.  233rd Field Coy. R.E.
 "   "    3.  237th Field Coy. R.E.
 "   "    4.  19th Bn. Middlesex Regt.
 "   "    5.  41st Division "G"          )
 "   "    6.  41st Division "Q"          )
 "   "    7.  122nd Infantry Brigade.    )
 "   "    8.  123rd Infantry Brigade.    ) for information.
 "   "    9.  124th Infantry Brigade.    )
 "   "   10.  C.R.E. 42nd Division.      )
 "   "   11.  C.E. XVth Corps.           )
 "   "   12.  C.R.E. 41st Division.
```

S E C R E T.　　　　　　　　　　　　　COPY NO. 8

C.R.E.'s OPERATION ORDER C.S. No.2.

9th October, 1917.

1. The Divisional Programme of Work

   (a) In the forward area.
   (b) In the COXYDE BAINS - OOST DUNKERKE area.
   (c) In the ST IDESBALDE - LA PANNE area

are forwarded for guidance.

2. Sundays will be observed as a day of rest by the Companies engaged in Hutting Work, and the Companies engaged in the forward area will arrange for the men to have one day in eight by roster for bathing and rest at the Waggon Lines.

                              E.M.Hockley,
                              Lieut. Colonel R.E.
                              C.R.E. 41st Division.

| Copy No. | | |
|---|---|---|
| 1. | 228th Field Coy. R.E. | |
| 2. | 233rd Field Coy. R.E. | |
| 3. | 237th Field Coy. R.E. | |
| 4. | 19th Bn. Middlesex Regt. | |
| 5. | 41st Division "G". | ) |
| 6. | 41st Division "Q". | ) |
| 7. | C.R.A. 42nd Division. | ) |
| 8. | 122nd Infantry Brigade. | ) for information. |
| 9. | 123rd Infantry Brigade. | ) |
| 10. | 124th Infantry Brigade. | ) |
| 11. | C.E. XVth Corps. | ) |
| 12. | C.R.E. 41st Division. | |

## PROGRAMME OF WORK IN FORWARD AREA EAST OF OOST DUNKERKE - OOST DUNKERKE BAINS ROAD.

233rd Field Coy. R.E. with working parties from Brigade in line.

1. M.G. Emplacement at HURL BISE and M.G. Emplacement and dugout at M.26.b.25.80.

2. M.G. dugouts at M.20.b.45.95. - M.20.d.2.4. and under Railway Embankment.

3. Strutting cellars in NIEUPORT BAINS.

4. Screening and signboarding in forward area.

5. Fixing bunks in accommodation tunnels as completed.

6. Gas proof doors for the cellars and dugouts.

7. Return to Waggon Lines at COXYDE BAINS for overhaul, sorting and repair all bridging material in the forward area.

8. Lateral trenches across NIEUPORT BAINS, viz: Left Reserve, BLIGHTY ALLEY, Left Support and "T" heads to be fire stepped at intervals, provided with Machine gun or Lewis gun loopholes firing down the streets or openings, and wired in front. The wire should not be continuous and gaps should be left to allow our troops to advance.

9. A short trench for riflemen on far side of Railway Embankment to fire over the foreshore - approach to be by sap. Sap and trench to be carefully camouflaged.

10. More wire is required in front of front line and on the flank of the Communication Trenches leading to BEACON TRENCH. These Communication Trenches must nbe strengthened and fire-stepped.

11. The Communication Trenches and trenches forming the Right Defensive Flank require improving and strengthening.

12. The Support Trench behind the Railway Embankment to be improved and provided with a parados.

13. The Reserve Line requires connecting up. The right posts in M.20.d. require thickening. At present they are not bullet proof.

"C" Coy. 19th Bn. Middlesex Regt.

1. Maintenance of roads forward of the OOST DUNKERKE - OOST DUNKERKE BAINS roads.

2. Maintenance of the Trench Tramway System from the connection with Light Railway at Nos. 1 & 2 Advanced Dumps and re-organisation of the whole system with 20 lbs. rail for use of 3 ton trucks.

"D" Coy. 19th. Bn. Middlesex Regt.

1. Maintenance and improvement of Communication tracks, boyeaux and trenches.

PROGRAMME OF HUTTING WORK WEST OF THE
COXYDE - COXYDE BAINS ROAD.

228th Field Coy. R.E. and "A" Coy. 19th Bn.
Middlesex Regt. with working parties from
Reserve Brigade

1. Brigade Transport Lines about ST IDESBALDE

    (a) Battalion at about W.10.b.9.4.
    (b)     "         "    "  W.11.c.2.8.
    (c)     "         "    "  W.11.c.7.5.
    (d)     "         "    "  W.11.d.3.7.

    each Transport Lines to consist of two 30 horse
    stables, 5 Nissen Huts of 20 men in each,
    Quartermaster's store, 1 Nissen Hut for Qr.Mr.
    and Transport Officer, cookhouse, ablution room
    and latrines.

2. D.H.Q. transport Lines at about W.10.c.5.8.

3. Field Ambulance Transport Lines at about W.16.b.2.7.

4. Artillery Wagon Lines in the LA PANNE Area

    (a) One Battery R.F.A. at W.20.b.7.6.
    (b)  "     "      "   "  W.20.b.3.5.
    (c)  "     "      "   "  W.20.a.7.5.
    (d)  "     "      "   "  W.20.a.7.2.
    (e)  "     "      "   "  W.16.d.4.3.
    (f)  "     "      "   "  W.16.d.4.3.
    (g) One Section D.A.C. "  W.21.a.2.6.
        (work suspended. New site to be selected)

PROGRAMME OF HUTTING AND DEFENCE WORK
EAST OF COXYDE – COXYDE BAINS ROAD.
------------------------------  ------------------------------

237th Field Coy. R.E. and "B" Coy. 19th Bn.
Middlesex Regt. with working parties from
Support Brigade and units concerned.

1. Completion of advanced Divl. Hd.Qrs. at R.27.c.5.3.
   and strutting of access trenches.

2. Technical assistance to R.F.A. in constructing
   Battery positions including gas-proofing of
   dugouts.

3. Technical assistance to units in the area in
   providing splinter proof shelter for huts and
   stables and improvement of accommodation.

4. Reinforcing cellars and billets in OOST DUNKERKE
   BAINS and provision of gas-proof doors.

5. Wiring machine gun emplacements in the AEOLIAN
   Road line in accordance with plan ~~proposed~~ *prepared* by
   XVth Corps.

SECRET.                                                        COPY NO. 9

C.R.E'S OPERATION ORDER C.S. No.2.
-------------------------------------

                                                   11th October, 1917.

1. The 228th and 237th Field Coys. will be struck off all
   other duties for Bridging Practice with effect from the
   12th instant.

2. The Work allotted on the Divisional programme to these
   companies will be temporarily taken over by "A" and "B"
   Companies 19th Bn. Middlesex Regt respectively and any
   further winter accommodation work held in abeyance.

3. The 228th Field Coy. with attached infantry will practise
   Berthon boat rafting; rowing and ferrying on the canal
   at Sheet 19.N.E. E.2.d.4.2. The Berthon boat equipment
   at WINCHESTER DUMP will be taken over and stores at site
   of practise: and a guard mounted. The Company will work
   from present billets in LA PANNE.

4. The 237th Field Coy. with attached infantry will practise
   medium and light pontoon bridging and barrel piering on
   the canal at Sheet 19.N.E. D.11.d.1.5.  42 pontoons from
   the Mechanical Bridging Train will be sent to this site.

   The 237th Field Coy. less one section at work sorting and
   repairing bridging stores at NIEUPORT BAINS and less
   pontoons and tool carts will move to camp at D.17.b.4.4.
   on the 12th instant.

5. ACKNOWLEDGE.

                                                   Lieut. Colonel R.E.

                                                   C.R.E. 41st Division.


Copy No. 1.  228th Field Coy. R.E.
 "   "   2.  233rd Field Coy. R.E.
 "   "   3.  237th Field Coy. R.E.
 "   "   4.  19th Bn. Middlesex Regt.
 "   "   5.  41st Division "G"        )
 "   "   6.  41st Division "         )
 "   "   7.  C.R.A. 41st Division.    )
 "   "   8.  122nd Infantry Brigade.  )
 "   "   9.  123rd Infantry Brigade.  ) for information.
 "   "  10.  124th Infantry Brigade.  )
 "   "  11.  C.E., XVth Corps.        )
 "   "  12.  C.R.E. 41st Division.

SECRET.   COPY NO. 8

C.R.E'S OPERATION ORDER C.S. No.4.

11th October, 1917.

1. With a view to reconnaissance and practise the attached preliminary distribution of R.E. and Pioneers in connection with operations for the crossing of the River YSER near its mouth and the establishment of a bridgehead East of the River is forwarded for guidance with map showing proposed crossings.

2. The pontoons for use by the 233rd Field Coy. R.E. will be the six divisional pontoons.

3. The pontoons for use by the 237th Field Coy. R.E. will be supplied by the Mechanical Pontoon Park.

4. ACKNOWLEDGE.

F.M.Mockler
Lieut. Colonel R.E.
C.R.E. 41st Division.

Copy No. 1. 228th Field Coy. R.E.
"    " 2. 233rd Field Coy. R.E.
"    " 3. 237th Field Coy. R.E.
"    " 4. 19th Bn. Middlesex Regt.
"    " 5. 41st Division "G"
"    " 6. 41st Division "Q"
"    " 7. C.R.A. 41st Division.
"    " 8. 122nd Infantry Brigade.
"    " 9. 123rd Infantry Brigade.
"    " 10. 124th Infantry Brigade.
"    " 11. C.E. XVth Corps.
"    " 12. C.R.E. 41st Division.

APPENDIX 1.

## DISTRIBUTION OF DIVISIONAL ENGINEERS FOR OPERATIONS.

| UNIT. | STRENGTH. | POSITION ON "Y" DAY. | WORK. |
|---|---|---|---|
| 237th Fld. Coy. R.E. | 4 sections & 550 att. infantry. | SURREY CAMP. | Pontoon Bridge at site of old MORTLAKE BRIDGE. |
| | | | Pontoon Bridge at site of RICHMOND BRIDGE as soon as 4 pontoons have been launched. (Work to proceed concurrently) |
| | | | Barrel bridge on up stream side of NEW MORTLAKE BRIDGE. |
| | | | Barrel bridge near NEW RICHMOND BRIDGE. |
| 235rd Fld. Coy.R.E. | 2 sections & 60 att. infantry. | Billets at NIEUPORT BAINS. | Ferrying 4 pontoons near site of Old RICHMOND BRIDGE (No.1 crossing) |
| | 1 section | do. | In Company Reserve. |
| | 1 section & 100 att. infantry. | do. | Consolidation of Strong Points on East side of River YSER. |
| 228th Fld Coy. R.E. | 4 sections & ½ Coy. Pnrs. | SURREY CAMP. | Ferrying 1 boat and 1 double Berthon raft at M.15.c.1,2. (No.8.crossing) |
| | | | Ferrying 1 boat and 1 double Berthon raft at M.14.d.8.4. (No.7 crossing) |
| | | | Ferrying 1 boat and 2 double Berthon rafts at M.14.d.5.8. (No.6 crossing) |
| A Fld.Co. to be detailed. | 2 sections) 2 sections) | Billets at OOST DUNKERKE -BAINS. | Maintenance of completed bridges. Divisional reserve. |
| 19th Bn. Middx.Rgt. (Pioneers) | ½ Coy. | KENT CAMP. | Maintenance of roads, filling shell holes & keeping roads open for traffic. |
| | ½ Coy. | | Maintenance of tramways. |
| | ¼ Coy. | | Maintenance of subways & Communication trenches. |
| | ¼ Coy. | | Assist 228th Field Coy. R.E. on Ferries (see above) |

APPENDIX 1 (Contd)

| UNIT. | STRENGTH. | POSITION ON "Y" DAY. | WORK. |
|---|---|---|---|
| 19th Bn. Middx. Regt.(Pnrs) | 1 Coy. | KENT CAMP. | Construction of tracks on E.side of R.YSER. |
| | 1 Coy. | | Divisional reserve. |
| 2nd Austln. Tunnelling Coy. | 1 section. | Billets at COXYDE-BAINS V.6.a.8.4. | Construction of wells on E.side of R. YSER. |
| | 1 section. | | On maintenance of following subways - BATH AVENUE and BATH LANE from ZERO. |
| | 2 sections. | | Divisional reserve. |

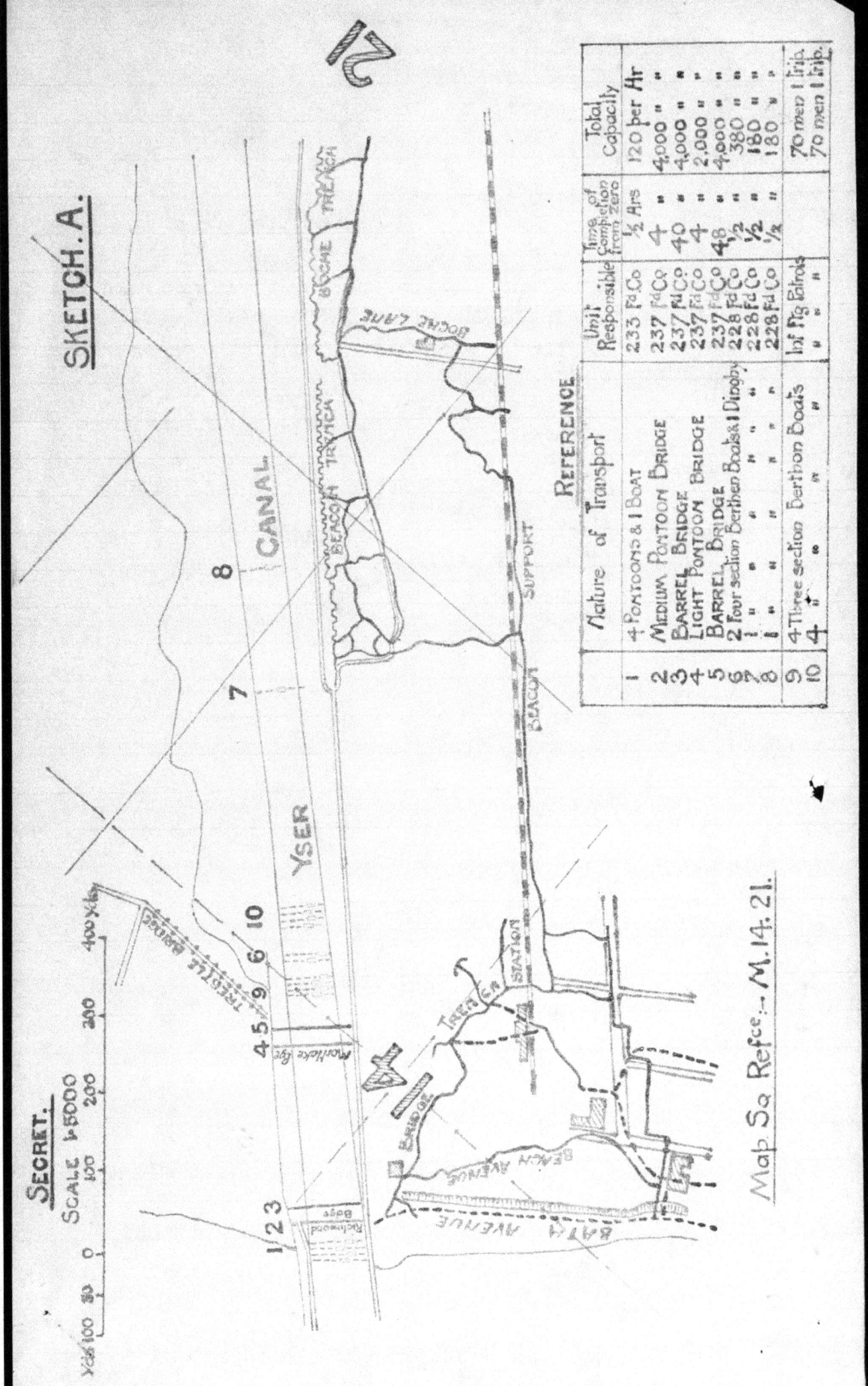

www.ingramcontent.com/pod-product-compliance
Lightning Source LLC
Chambersburg PA
CBHW081547160426
43191CB00011B/1857